Scope of Total Architecture

WORLD PERSPECTIVES

Planned and Edited by Ruth Nanda Anshen

FIRST TITLES

JACQUES MARITAIN
Approaches to God

KONRAD ADENHAUER
World Indivisible

RADHAKRISHNAN
Recovery of Faith

BROCK CHISHOLM
Can Nations Learn to Learn?

LEWIS MUMFORD
The Transformation of Man

WORLD PERSPECTIVES

WALTER GROPIUS

Scope of
Total
Architecture

GEORGE ALLEN & UNWIN LTD
RUSKIN HOUSE
MUSEUM STREET LONDON

First published in Great Britain in 1956

Printed in Great Britain
in 11 Point Pilgrim Type
by East Midland Allied Press, Ltd.,
Kettering, Peterborough and elsewhere

World Perspectives

World Perspectives is dedicated to the concept of man born out of a universe perceived through a fresh vision of reality. Its aim is to present short books written by the most conscious and responsible minds of today. Each volume represents the thought and belief of each author and sets forth the interrelation of the changing religious, scientific, artistic, political, economic and social influences upon man's total experience.

This Series is committed to a re-examination of all those sides of human endeavour which the specialist was taught to believe he could safely leave aside. It interprets present and past events impinging on human life in our growing World Age and envisages what man may yet attain when summoned by an unbending inner necessity to the quest of what is most exalted in him. Its purpose is to offer new vistas in terms of world and human development while refusing to betray the intimate correlation between universality and individuality, dynamics and form, freedom and destiny. Each author treats his subject from the broad perspective of the world community, not from the Judaeo-Christian, Western, or Eastern viewpoint alone.

Certain fundamental questions which have received too little consideration in the face of the spiritual, moral and political world crisis of our day, and in the light of technology which has released the creative energies of peoples, are treated in these books. Our authors deal with the increasing realisation that spirit and nature are not separate and apart; that intuition and reason must regain their importance as the means of perceiving and fusing inner being with outer reality.

Knowledge, it is shown, no longer consists in a manipulation of man and nature as opposite forces, nor in the reduction of data to mere statistical order, but is a means of liberating mankind from the destructive power of fear, pointing the way toward the goal of the rehabilitation of the human will and the rebirth of faith and confidence in the human person. The works published also endeavour to reveal that the cry for patterns, systems and authorities is growing less insistent as the desire grows stronger in both East and West for the recovery of a dignity, integrity and self-realisation which are the inalienable rights of man who may now guide change by means of conscious purpose in the light of rational experience.

Other vital questions explored relate to problems of international understanding as well as to problems dealing with prejudice and the resultant tensions and antagonisms. The growing perception and responsibility of our World Age point to the new reality that the individual person and the collective person supplement and integrate each other; that the thrall of totalitarianism of both right and left has been shaken in the universal desire to recapture the authority of truth and of human totality. Mankind can finally p'ace its trust not in a proletarian authoritarianism, not in a secularised humanism, both of which have betrayed the spiritual property right of history, but in a sacramental brotherhood and in the unity of knowledge, a widening of human horizons beyond every parochialism, and a revolution in human thought comparable to the basic assumption, among the ancient Greeks, of the sovereignty of reason; corresponding to the great effulgence of the moral conscience articulated by the Hebrew prophets; analogous to the fundamental assertions of Christianity; or to the beginning of a new scientific era, the era of the science of dynamics, the experimental foundations of which were laid by Galileo in the Renaissance.

An important effort of this Series is to re-examine the contradictory meanings and applications which are given today to such terms as democracy, freedom, justice, love, peace, brotherhood and God. The purpose of such inquiries is to clear the way for the foundation of a genuine *world* history not in terms of nation or race or culture but in terms of man in relation to God, to himself, his fellow man and the universe, that reach beyond immediate self-interest. For the meaning of the World Age consists in respecting man's hopes and dreams which lead to a deeper understanding of the basic values of all peoples.

Today in the East and in the West men are discovering that they are bound together, beyond any divisiveness, by a more fundamental unity than any mere agreement in thought and doctrine. They are beginning to know that all men possess the same primordial desires and tendencies; that the domination of man over man can no longer be justified by any appeal to God or nature; and such consciousness is the fruit of the spiritual and moral revolution through which humanity is now passing.

World Perspectives is planned to gain insight into the meaning of man, who not only is determined by history but who also determines history. History is to be understood as concerned not only with the life of man on this planet but as including also such cosmic influences as interpenetrate our human world.

This generation is discovering that history does not conform to the social optimism of modern civilisation and that the organisation of human communities and the establishment of justice, freedom and peace are not only intellectual achievements but spiritual and moral achievements as well, demanding a cherishing of the wholeness of human personality and constituting a never-ending challenge to man, emerging from the abyss of meaninglessness and suffering, to be renewed and replenished in the totality of his life. 'For as one's thinking is, such one becomes, and it is because of this that thinking should be purified and transformed, for were it centred upon truth as it is now upon things perceptible to the senses, who would not be liberated from his bondage.'[1]

There is in mankind today a counterforce to the sterility and danger of a quantitative, anonymous mass culture, a new, if sometimes imperceptible, spiritual sense of convergence toward world unity on the basis of the sacredness of each human person and respect for the plurality of cultures. There is a growing awareness that equality and justice are not to be evaluated in mere numerical terms but that they are proportionate and analogical in their reality.

We stand at the brink of the age of the world in which human life presses forward to actualise new forms. The false

[1] *Maitri Upanishad* 6.34.4, 6.

separation of man and nature, of time and space, of freedom and security, is acknowledged and we are faced with a new vision of man in his organic unity and of history offering a richness and diversity of quality and majesty of scope hitherto unprecedented. In relating the accumulated wisdom of man's spirit to the new reality of the World Age, in articulating its thought and belief, *World Perspectives* seeks to encourage a renaissance of hope in society and of pride in man's decision as to what his destiny will be.

The experience of dread, in the pit of which contemporary man has been plunged through his failure to transcend his existential limits, is the experience of the problem of whether he shall attain to being through the knowledge of himself or shall not, whether he shall annihilate nothingness or whether nothingness shall annihilate him. For he has been forced back to his origins as a result of the atrophy of meaning, and his anabasis may begin once more through his mysterious greatness to re-create his life.

In spite of the infinite obligation of men and in spite of their finite power, in spite of the intransigence of nationalisms, and in spite of spiritual bereavement and moral denigration, beneath the apparent turmoil and upheaval of the present, and out of the transformations of this dynamic period with the unfolding of a world-consciousness, the purpose of *World Perspectives* is to help quicken the 'unshaken heart of well-rounded truth' and interpret the significant elements of the World Age now taking shape out of the core of that undimmed continuity of the creative process which restores man to mankind while deepening and enhancing his communion with the universe.

New York, 1955   RUTH NANDA ANSHEN

Preface

Creation and love of beauty are elemental for the experience of happiness. A time which does not recognise this basic truth does not become articulate in the visual sense; its image remains blurred, its manifestations fail to delight.

Since my early youth I have been acutely aware of the chaotic ugliness of our modern man-made environment when compared to the unity and beauty of old, pre-industrial towns. In the course of my life I became more and more convinced that the usual practice of architects to relieve the dominating disjointed pattern here and there by a beautiful building is most inadequate and that we must find, instead, a new set of values, based on such constituent factors as would generate an integrated expression of the thought and feeling of our time.

How such a unity might be attained to become the visible pattern for a true democracy—that is the topic of this book. It is based, essentially, on articles and lectures written—with a few exceptions—during my years in Harvard University as Chairman of the Department of Architecture (1937-1952).*

WALTER GROPIUS

* Acknowledgment: The idea to publish this book originated with my wife, Ise, née Frank, who undertook to edit and select the material from my manuscripts.

Contents

Illustrations

Introduction*

Entering a new chapter in my life that—contrary to the normal expectation of life after seventy—looks to me just as turbulent and perilous as the period preceding it, I realise that I am a figure covered with labels, maybe to the point of obscurity. Names like 'Bauhaus Style,' 'International Style,' 'Functional Style' have almost succeeded in hiding the human core behind it all, and I am eager, therefore, to put a few cracks into this dummy that busy people have slipped around me.

When, as a young man, I received the first public attention I was rather put out to find my mother depressed and disapproving of the fact that my name had begun to appear in newspapers. Today I understand her apprehension all too well, because I have experienced that, in our era of fast printing and categorising, publicity is likely to be tied round an individual like a label around a bottle. Every so often I feel a strong urge to shake off this growing crust so that the man behind the tag and the label may become visible again.

I have been told that a tree which is supposed to bear my name is to be planted in Chicago on the campus of the Michael Reese Hospital, for which I have been architectural consultant for the last eight years. I want this to be a tree in which birds of many colours and shapes can sit and feel sustained. I do not wish to restrict it to species with square tail-ends or streamlined contours or international features or Bauhaus garb. In short, I wish it to be a hospitable tree from which many songs should be heard, except the fake sounds of the bird imitators.

When I was a small boy somebody asked me what my favourite colour was. For years my family poked fun at me for saying, after some hesitation, *'Bunt ist meine Lieblingsfarbe,'* meaning: 'Multicoloured is my favourite colour.' The strong

* From a speech made by the author on the occasion of his seventieth birthday on invitation of the Illinois Institute of Technology, Chicago, May, 1953.

desire to *include* every vital component of life instead of excluding part of them for the sake of too narrow and dogmatic an approach has characterised my whole life. It is, therefore, with considerable disgust that I have watched the confusing battle of words that has arisen around the representatives of the various schools of modern design. These aesthetic battles are usually not stirred up by the architects themselves, but by those well-meaning or ill-meaning, self-appointed critics who, in the attempt to buttress their own aesthetic or political theories, wreak havoc with the work of creative people by capturing and abusing some of their statements without comprehending the background and context they sprang from.

I have found throughout my life that words and, particularly, theories not tested by experience, can be much more harmful than deeds. When I came to the U.S.A. in 1937 I enjoyed the tendency among Americans to go straight to the practical test of every new-born idea, instead of snipping off every new shoot by excessive and premature debate over its possible value, a bad habit that frustrates so many efforts in Europe. This great quality should not get lost in favour of biased theorising and fruitless, garrulous controversy at a moment when we need to muster all our strength and originality in trying to keep creative impulses active and effective against the deadening effect of mechanisation and overorganisation that is threatening our society.

Of course, the relative position which a searching mind has to take when going off the beaten path exposes it to attacks from all directions. In my time I have been accused by the Nazis of being a Red, by the Communists of being a typical exponent of the capitalistic society, and by some Americans of being a 'foreigner,' unacquainted with the democratic way of life. All these labels, applied to the same person, show the confusion that is caused in our time by an individual who just insisted on forming his own conviction. I look upon these temporary tempests in my personal life with the detachment that comes from experience. I know that the strong currents of our times might have cast my boat on the rocks many times unless I could have trusted my own compass.

But the thing I do not want to seem detached about is our

common plight of losing control over the vehicle of progress that our time has created and that is beginning to ride rough-shod over our lives. I mean that the misuse of the machine is creating a soul-flattening mass-mind, which levels off individual diversity and independence of thought and action. Diversity is, after all, the very source of true democracy. But factors of expediency like high-pressure salesmanship, organisational oversimplification and moneymaking as an end in itself have surely impaired the individual's capacity to seek and understand the deeper potentialities of life.

Democracy is based on the interplay of two contrasting manifestations. On the one hand it needs diversity of minds, resulting from intensive, individual performance; on the other it needs a common denominator of regional expression, springing from the cumulative experience of successive generations who gradually weed out the merely arbitrary from the essential and typical. As irreconcilable as these two manifestations may seem to be, I believe that their fusion can and must be brought about or we shall end up as robots.

One of the U.S. Supreme Court Justices once discussed the substance of democratic procedure and I was highly interested to hear him define it as 'essentially a matter of *degree*.' He did not base his decisions on abstract principles of right and wrong, but wanted to consider every case in its particular circumstances and relative proportion, because he felt that it was the soundness of the whole social structure that mattered and that what might contribute to its detriment today might be inconsequential tomorrow under changing conditions, and vice versa.

To sharpen this sense of balance and feeling for equipoise is something we all have to accomplish individually in our lives. For instance, when we accuse technology and science of having deranged our previous concepts of beauty and the 'good life,' we would do well to remember that it is not the bewildering profusion of technical mass-production machinery that is dictating the course of events, but the inertia or the alertness of our brain that gives or neglects to give direction to this development. For example, our generation has been guilty of producing horrors of repetitious housing developments, all done on a handicraft basis, which can easily compete in deadly uniformity with those ill-advised prefabrication systems which multiply the whole house instead of only its component parts. It is not the tool, it is our mind that is at fault. The art of accurately knowing the degree to which our individual instincts are to be curbed or encouraged or our common policies enforced or resisted is apparently the privilege of few wise people, and we are desperately in need of them. No other generation has had to face so vast a panorama of conflicting tendencies and our heritage of over-specialisation does not equip us too well to cope with them. The architecture we produce will inevitably reveal the degree to which we have been able to show respect for the developing social pattern which we are part of, without devitalising our individual contribution to it.

I want to rip off at least one of the misleading labels that I and others have been decorated with. There is no such thing as an 'International Style,' unless you want to speak of certain universal technical achievements in our period which belong to the intellectual equipment of every civilised nation, or unless you want to speak to those pale examples of what I call 'applied archeology,' which you find among the public buildings from Moscow to Madrid to Washington. Steel or concrete skeletons, ribbon windows, slabs cantilevered or wings hovering on stilts are but impersonal contemporary means—the raw stuff, so to speak—with which regionally different architectural manifestations can be created. The constructive achievements of the Gothic period—its vaults, arches, buttresses and pinnacles—similarly became a common international experience. Yet, what a great regional variety of architectural expression has resulted from it in the different countries !

As to my practice, when I built my first house in the U.S.A. —which was my own—I made it a point to absorb into my own conception those features of the New England architectural tradition that I found still alive and adequate. This fusion of the regional spirit with a contemporary approach to design produced a house that I would never have built in Europe with its entirely different climatic, technical and psychological background.

I tried to face the problem in much the same way as the early builders of the region had faced it when, with the best technical means at their disposal, they built unostentatious, clearly defined buildings that were able to withstand the rigours of the climate and that expressed the social attitude of their inhabitants.

Our present responsibility seems to be to determine which features of our vast industrial civilisation represent the best and lasting values and should therefore be cultivated to form the nucleus for a new tradition. Proper distinction of cultural values can, of course, develop only through steadily improved education. One of the major jobs falling to us architects in the field of cultural education would be to point up and make precise the new values and sift them from the welter of ascending and fading fashions and a mass production process that has yet to discover that change, as such, does not necessarily bring improvement. Amidst a vast production and an almost limitless choice of goods and types of all description, we need to remember that cultural standards result from a selective process of seeking out the essential and typical. This voluntary limitation, far from producing dull uniformity, should give many individuals a chance to contribute their own individual variation of a common theme and so help to evolve again the integrated pattern for living that we abandoned with the advent of the machine age. The two opposites—individual variety and a common denominator for all—will then once more be reconciled to each other.

WALTER GROPIUS

I

Education of Architects and Designers

Approach[*]

My intention is not to introduce a, so to speak, cut and dried 'Modern Style' from Europe, but rather to introduce a method of approach which allows one to tackle a problem according to its peculiar conditions. I want a young architect to be able to find his way in whatever circumstances; I want him independently to create true, genuine forms out of the technical, economic and social conditions in which he finds himself instead of imposing a learned formula on to surroundings which may call for an entirely different solution. It is not so much a ready-made dogma that I want to teach, but an attitude toward the problems of our generation which is unbiased, original and elastic. It would be an absolute horror for me if my appointment would result in the multiplication of a fixed idea of 'Gropius architecture.' What I do want is to make young people realise how inexhaustible the means of creation are if they make use of the innumerable modern products of our age, and to encourage these young people in finding their own solutions.

I have sometimes felt a certain disappointment at being asked only for the facts and tricks in my work when my interest was in handing on my basic experiences and underlying methods. In learning the facts and tricks, some can obtain sure results in a comparatively short time, of course; but these results are superficial and unsatisfactory because they still leave the student helpless if he is faced with a new and unexpected situation. If he has not been trained to get an insight into organic development no skilful addition of modern motives, however elaborate, will enable him to do creative work.

[*] From a statement, made for *The Architectural Record*, at the start of my teaching career as Professor of Architecture at Harvard University, May, 1937.

My ideas have often been interpreted as the peak of rationalisation and mechanisation. This gives quite a wrong picture of my endeavours. I have always emphasised that the other aspect, the satisfaction of the human soul, is just as important as the material, and that the achievement of a new spatial vision means more than structural economy and functional perfection. The slogan 'fitness for purpose equals beauty' is only half true. When do we call a human face beautiful? Every face is fit for purpose in its parts, but only perfect proportions and colours in a well balanced harmony deserve that title of honour: beautiful. Just the same is true in architecture. Only perfect harmony in its technical functions as well as in its proportions can result in beauty. That makes our task so manifold and complex.

More than ever before is it in the hands of us architects to help our contemporaries to lead a natural and sensible life instead of paying a heavy tribute to the false gods of make-believe. We can respond to this demand only if we are not afraid to approach our work from the broadest possible angle. *Good architecture should be a projection of life itself and that implies an intimate knowledge of biological, social, technical and artistic problems*. But then—even that is not enough. To make a unity out of all these different branches of human activity, a strong character is required and that is where the means of education partly come to an end. Still, it should be our highest aim to produce this type of men who are able to visualise an entity rather than let themselves get absorbed too early into the narrow channels of specialisation. Our century has produced the expert type in millions; let us make way now for the men of vision.

My Conception of the Bauhaus Idea*

AIM. After I had already found my own ground in architecture before the First World War, as is evidenced in the Fagus Building of 1911 and in the Cologne Werkbund Exhibition in 1914, the full consciousness of my responsibility as an architect, based on my own reflections, came to me as a result of the First World War, during which my theoretical premises first took shape.

After that violent eruption, every thinking man felt the necessity for an intellectual change of front. Each in his own particular sphere of activity aspired to help in bridging the disastrous gulf between realism and idealism. It was then that the immensity of the mission of the architect of my own generation first dawned on me. I saw that, first of all, a new scope for architecture had to be outlined, which I could not hope to realise, however, by my own architectural contributions alone, but which would have to be achieved by training and preparing a new generation of architects in close contact with modern means of production in a pilot school which must succeed in acquiring authoritative significance.

I saw also that to make this possible would require a whole staff of collaborators and assistants, men who would work, not as an orchestra obeying the conductor's baton, but independently, although in close co-operation to further a common cause. Consequently I tried to put the emphasis of my work on integration and co-ordination, inclusiveness, not exclusiveness, for I felt that the art of building is contingent upon the co-ordinated teamwork of a band of active collaborators whose

* See : *The New Architecture and the Bauhaus* by W. Gropius, Faber & Faber, London, 1935. 'Education towards Creative Design' by W. Gropius, *American Architect and Architecture*, New York, May 1937. 'The Gropius Symposium' in *The American Academy of Arts and Sciences, Arts and Architecture*, California, May, 1952.

co-operation symbolises the co-operative organism of what we call society.

Thus the Bauhaus was inaugurated in 1919 with the specific object of realising a modern architectonic art, which like human nature was meant to be all-embracing in its scope. It deliberately concentrated primarily on what has now become a work of imperative urgency—averting mankind's enslavement by the machine by saving the mass-product and the home from mechanical anarchy and by restoring them to purpose, sense and life. This means evolving goods and buildings specifically designed for industrial production. Our object was to eliminate the drawbacks of the machine without sacrificing any one of its real advantages. We aimed at realising standards of excellence, not creating transient novelties. Experiment once more became the centre of architecture, and that demands a broad, co-ordinating mind, not the narrow specialist.

What the Bauhaus preached in practice was the common citizenship of all forms of creative work, and their logical interdependence on one another in the modern world. Our guiding principle was that design is neither an intellectual nor a material affair, but simply an integral part of the stuff of life, necessary for everyone in a civilised society. Our ambition was to rouse the creative artist from his other-worldliness and to reintegrate him into the workaday world of realities and, at the same time, to broaden and humanise the rigid, almost exclusively material mind of the businessman. Our conception of the basic unity of all design in relation to life was in diametric opposition to that of 'art for art's sake' and the much more dangerous philosophy it sprang from, business as an end in itself.

This explains our concentration on the design of technical products and the organic sequence of their processes of manufacture, which gave rise to an erroneous idea that the Bauhaus had set itself up as the apotheosis of rationalism. In reality, however, we were far more preoccupied with exploring the territory that is common to the formal and technical spheres, and defining where they cease to coincide. The standardisation of the practical machinery of life implies no robotisation of the individual but, on the contrary, the unburdening of his existence from much unnecessary dead weight so as to leave him freer to develop on a higher plane.

All too often, our real intentions have been and still are misunderstood, namely, to see in the movement an attempt at creating a 'style' and to identify every building and object in which ornament and period style seem to be discarded as examples of an imaginary 'Bauhaus Style.' This is contrary to what we were aiming at. *The object of the Bauhaus was not to propagate any 'style,' system or dogma, but simply to exert a revitalising influence on design.* A 'Bauhaus Style' would have been a confession of failure and a return to that devitalising inertia, that stagnating academism which I had called it into being to combat. Our endeavours were to find a new approach which would promote a creative state of mind in those taking part and which would finally lead to a new attitude toward life. To my knowledge, the Bauhaus was the first institution in the world to dare to embody this principle in a definite curriculum. The conception of this curriculum was preceded by an analysis of the conditions of our industrial period and its compelling trends.

ARTS AND CRAFT SCHOOLS. When, in the last century, the machine-made products seemed to sweep the world, leaving the craftsmen and artists in a bad plight, a natural reaction gradually set in against the abandonment of form and the submersion of quality. Ruskin and Morris were the first to set their faces against the tide, but their opposition against the machine could not stem the waters. It was only much later that the perplexed mind of those interested in the development of form realised that art and production can be reunited only by accepting the machine and subjugating it to the mind. 'The Arts and Crafts' schools for 'applied art' arose mainly in Germany, but most of them met the demand only halfway, as their training was too superficial and technically amateurish to bring about a real advance. The manufactories still continued to turn out masses of ill-shaped goods while the artist struggled in vain to supply platonic designs. The trouble was that neither of them succeeded in penetrating far enough into the realm of the other to accomplish an effective fusion of both their endeavours.

The craftsman, on the other hand, with the passing of time began to show only a faint resemblance to the vigorous and independent representative of medieval culture who had been in full command of the whole production of his time and who had been a technician, an artist and a merchant combined. His workshop turned into a shop, the working process slipped out of his hand and the craftsman became a merchant. The complete individual, bereaved of the creative part of his work, thus degenerated into a partial being. His ability to train and instruct his disciples began to vanish and the young apprentices gradually moved into factories. There they found themselves surrounded by a meaningless mechanisation which blunted their creative instincts, and their pleasure in their own work; their inclination to learn disappeared rapidly.

DIFFERENCE BETWEEN HANDICRAFTS AND MACHINE WORK. What is the reason for this devitalising process? What is the difference between handicraft and machine work? *The difference between industry and handicraft is due far less to the different nature of the tools employed in each, than to sub-division of labour in the one and undivided control by a single workman in the other.* This compulsory restriction of personal initiative is the threatening cultural danger of the present-day form of industry. The only remedy is a completely changed attitude toward work which, though based on the sensible realisation that the development of technique has shown how a collective form of labour can lead humanity to greater total efficiency than the autocratic labour of the isolated individual, should not detract from the power and importance of personal effort. On the contrary, by giving it the possibility of taking its proper place in the work of the whole it will even enhance its practical effect. This attitude no longer perceives in the machine merely an economic means for dispensing with as many manual workers as possible and of depriving them of their livelihood, nor yet a means of imitating handwork; but, rather, an instrument which is to relieve man of the most oppressive physical labour and serve to strengthen his hand so as to enable him to give form to his creative impulse. The fact that we have not yet mastered the new means of production and, in consequence, still have to suffer from them, is not a valid argument against their necessity. The main problem will be to discover the most effective way of distributing the creative energies in the organisation as a whole. The intelligent craftsman of the past will in future become responsible for the speculative preliminary work in the production of industrial goods. Instead of being forced into mechanical machine work, his abilities must be used for laboratory and tool-making work and fused with the industry into a new working unit. At present the young artisan is, for economic reasons, forced either to descend to the level of a factory hand in industry or to become an organ for carrying into effect the platonic ideas of others; i.e., of the artist-designer. In no case does he any longer solve a problem of his own. With the help of the artist he produces goods with merely decorative nuances of new taste which, although associated with a sense of quality, lack any deep-rooted progress in the structural development, born of a knowledge of the new means of production.

What, then, must we do to give the rising generation a more promising approach to their future profession as designers, craftsmen or architects? What training establishments must we create in order to be able to sift out the artistically gifted person and fit him by extensive manual and mental training for independent creative work within the industrial production? Only in very isolated cases have training schools been established with the aim of turning out this new type of worker who is able to combine the qualities of an artist, a technician and a businessman. One of the attempts to regain contact with production and to train young students both for handwork and for machine work, and as designers at the same time, was made by the Bauhaus.

BAUHAUS TRAINING: PRELIMINARY COURSE. The Bauhaus aimed at the training of people possessing artistic talents as designers in industry and handicrafts, as sculptors, painters and architects. A complete co-ordinated training of all handicrafts, in technique and in form, with the object of teamwork in building, served as the basis. The fact that the man of today is, from the outset, left too much to traditional specialised training—which merely imparts to him a specialised knowledge, but does not make clear to him the meaning and purport of his work, nor the relationship in which he stands to the world at large—was counteracted at the Bauhaus by putting at the beginning of its training not the 'trade' but the 'human being' in his natural readiness to grasp life as a whole. The basis of its training was a preliminary course, introducing the pupil to the experience of proportion and scale, rhythm, light, shade and colour, and allowing him at the same time to pass through every stage of primitive experience with materials and tools of all kinds in order to enable him to find a place where, within the limits of his natural gifts, he could obtain a secure footing. This training, which occupied six months, was intended to develop and ripen intelligence, feeling and ideas, with the general object of evolving the 'complete being' who, from his biological centre, could approach all things of life with instinctive certainty and would no longer be taken unawares by the rush and convulsion of our 'Mechanical Age.' The objection that, in this world of industrial economy, such a general training implies extravagance or a loss of time does not, to my mind and experience, hold good. On the contrary, I have been able to observe that it not only gave the pupil greater confidence, but also considerably enhanced the productiveness and speed of his subsequent specialised training. Only when an understanding of the interrelationship of the phenomena of the world around him is awakened at an early age will he be able to incorporate his own personal share in the creative work of his time.

As both the future craftsman and the future artist were subject to the same fundamental training at the Bauhaus, it had to be sufficiently broad to enable each talent to find its own way. The concentric structure of the whole training embodied all the essential components of design and technique right from the beginning, in order to give the pupil an immediate insight into the whole field of his future activities. The further training merely gave breadth and depth; it differed from the elementary 'preliminary training' only in degree and thoroughness, but not in the essence. Simultaneously with the first exercises in materials and tools, the training in design commenced.

LANGUAGE OF VISION. In addition to technical and handicraft training, the designer must also learn a special language of shape in order to be able to give visible expression to his ideas. He has to absorb a scientific knowledge of objectively valid optical facts, a theory which guides the shaping hand and provides a general basis on which a multitude of individuals can work together harmoniously. This theory is naturally not a recipe for works of art, but it is the most important objective means for collective work in design. It can best be explained with an example from the musical world : the theory of counterpoint which, though in the course of time it may have undergone certain changes, is, neverthless, still a supraindividualistic system for regulating the world of tones. Its mastery is required lest the musical idea should remain lost in chaos ; for creative freedom does not reside in the infinitude of the means of expression and formation, but in free movement within its strictly legal bounds. The academy, whose task it had been from its beginning—when it was still a vital force—to tend and develop this theory for the optical arts, had failed because it lost touch with reality. Intensive studies were therefore made at the Bauhaus to rediscover this grammar of design in order to furnish the student with an objective knowledge of optical facts—such as proportion, optical illusions and colours. Careful cultivation and further investigation of these natural laws would do more to further true tradition than any instruction in the imitation of old forms and styles.

WORKSHOP TRAINING. In the course of his training, each student of the Bauhaus had to enter a workshop of his own choice, after having completed the preliminary course. There he studied simultaneously under two masters—one a handicraft master, and the other a master of design. This idea of starting with two different groups of teachers was a necessity, because neither artists possessing sufficient technical knowledge nor craftsmen endowed with sufficient imagination for artistic problems, who could have been made the leaders of the working departments, were to be found. A new generation capable of combining both these attributes had first to be trained. In later years, the Bauhaus succeeded in placing as masters in charge of the workshops former students who were then equipped with such equivalent technical and artistic experience that the separation of the staff into masters of form and masters of technique was found to be superfluous.

The training in handwork given in the Bauhaus workshops must not be taken as an end in itself, but as an irreplaceable means of education. The aim of this training was to produce designers who were able, by their intimate knowledge of materials and working processes, to influence the industrial production of our time. An attempt was made, therefore, to produce models for the industry which were not only designed but actually made in the workshops of the Bauhaus. The creation of standard types for the articles of daily use was their main concern. These workshops were essentially laboratories in which the models for such products were carefully evolved and constantly improved. Even though these models were made by hand, the model designers had to be fully acquainted with the methods of production on an industrial scale and so, during their training, the Bauhaus sent out its best students for a time, to do practical work in factories. Inversely, skilled workmen also came from the factories into the Bauhaus workshops, to discuss the needs of industry with masters and students. In this way a mutual influence arose which found its expression in valuable products, the technical and artistic quality of which were appreciated by manufacturer and customer.

DEVELOPMENT OF STANDARD TYPES. The creation of standard types for everyday goods is a social necessity. The standard product is by no means an invention of our own era. It is only the methods of producing it which have changed. It still implies the highest level of civilisation, the seeking out of the best, the separation of the essential and super-personal from the personal and accidental. It is today more necessary than ever to understand the underlying significance of the conception 'standard'—that is to say, as a cultural title of honour—and firmly to combat the shallow catchword propaganda which simply raises every industrial mass product to that high rank.

In its collaboration with industry, the Bauhaus attached special importance also to bringing the students into closer touch with economic problems. I am opposed to the erroneous view that the artistic abilities of a student may suffer by sharpening the sense of economy, time, money and material consumption. Obviously it is essential clearly to differentiate between the unrestricted work in a laboratory on which strict time limits can hardly be imposed, and work which has been ordered for completion at a certain date; that is to say, between the creative process of inventing a model and the technical process involved in its mass production. Creative ideas cannot be made to order, but the inventor of a model must nevertheless develop trained judgment of an economic method of subsequently manufacturing his model on mass production lines, even though time and consumption of material play only a subordinate part in the design and execution of the model itself.

The whole institution of the Bauhaus training shows the educational value which was attached to practical problems, which impel the students to overcome all internal and external friction. Collaboration on actual orders which the master had to execute was one of the outstanding advantages of handicrafts training in the Middle Ages. For that reason, I endeavoured to secure practical commissions for the Bauhaus, in which both masters and students could put their work to a test. In particular, the erection of our own institute buildings, in which the whole Bauhaus and its workshops co-operated, represented an ideal task. The demonstration of all kinds of new models made in our workshops, which we were able to show in practical use in the building, so thoroughly convinced manufacturers that they entered into royalty contracts with the Bauhaus which, as the turnover increased, proved a valuable source of revenue to the latter. The institution of obligatory practical work simultaneously afforded the possibility of paying students—even during their three years of training—for saleable articles and models which they had worked out. This provided many a capable student with some means of existence.

After a three-year training in handwork and design, the student had to submit to an examination both by the masters of the Bauhaus and by the 'Chamber of Handicrafts' in order to obtain the Journeyman's Certificate. The third stage for those who wanted to proceed was the building training. Co-operation on practical building sites, practical experiments with new building materials, studies in draughtsmanship and engineering in addition to design led to the Master Certificate of the Bauhaus. The students then became either practical architects or collaborators in the industry, or teachers—according to their special gifts. The thorough manual training in the workshops served as a very valuable equipment for those students who found it impossible to penetrate into the more comprehensive and complex task of the architect's profession. The gradual and manifold instruction of the Bauhaus enabled him to concentrate on precisely that kind of work which best suited his capabilities.

The most essential factor of the Bauhaus work was the fact that, with the passing of time, a certain homogeneity was evolved in all products: this came about as the result of the consciously developed spirit of collaborative work, and also in spite of the co-operation of the most divergent personalities and individualities. It was not based on external stylistic features, but rather on the effort to design things simply and truthfully in accordance with their intrinsic laws. The shapes which its products have assumed are therefore not a new fashion, but the result of clear reflection and innumerable processes of thought and work in a technical, economic and form-giving direction. The individual alone cannot attain this goal; only the collaboration of many can succeed in finding solutions which transcend the individual aspect—which will retain their validity for many years to come.

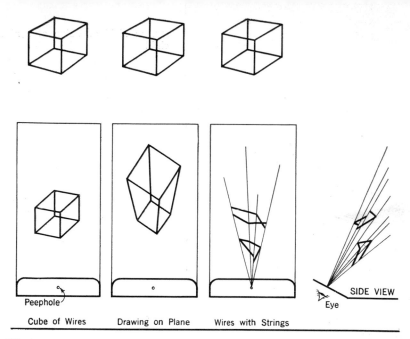

Peephole

Cube of Wires   Drawing on Plane   Wires with Strings

SIDE VIEW

Eye

FIG. 1

FIG. 2 : Plaza at entry of Chateau de Versailles

FIG. 3 : Field of vision of a nine-m... child

FIG. 4 : Photographic camera and the human eye

I   II

FIG. 5 :   A co... delusion

Accommodation apparatus

Lens

Vitreous Body

Accommodation apparatus

Sclera

Vascular Membrane

Pigment Layer

Retina

Optic Nerve

FIG. 6: Diagrammatic section through the human eye

FIG. 7: View into a human eye

: The adjustment of the human

: The iris diaphragm of the a and that of the human eye

FIG. 10 : The television apparatus of human eye

FIG. 11 : The human eye, a combination camera for day and night photography

FIG. 12 : Concavities of a moon land

FIG. 13 : The same picture upside d

FIG. 14

FIG. 16: Interior of Cathedral in Sienna

15: Girl in bathing suit

FIG. 17: Phenomenon of irradiation

FIG. 18: St. John in Lateran, Rome

FIG. 19 : El Greco's 'Grand Inquisitor'

FIG. 20 : Analysis of Greco's pictur (Bauhaus exercise)

FIG. 21 :
Relativity
of values

FIG. 22 : The size of our body is our yardstic

FIG. 23 : Egyptian sphinx

FIG. 24 : Westminster Cathedral

IG. 25 : Indian Temple

IG. 26 : Indian Temple, close view

FIG. 27 : Left, Indian cornice. Right, Baroque cornice

FIG. 28 : Plinth of the Parthe[non] Temple

FIG. 29 : Picture by Balla, Italy, depicting motion in space

FIG. 30 : Picture by Picass[o] depicting profile and front o[f] woman's face

THE CREATIVE TEACHER. The success of any idea depends upon the personal attributes of those responsible for carrying it out. The selection of the right teacher is the decisive factor in the results obtained by a training institute. Their personal attributes as men play an even more decisive part than their technical knowledge and ability, for it is upon the personal characteristics of the master that the success of fruitful collaboration with youth primarily depends. *If men of outstanding artistic ability are to be won for an institute, they must from the outset be afforded wide possibilities for their own further development by giving them time and space for private work.* The mere fact that such men continue to develop their own work in the institute produces that creative atmosphere which is so essential for a school of design and in which youthful talents can develop. This is the most important supposition, to which all other questions affecting the organisation must be subordinated. There is nothing more deadening to the vitality of a design school than when its teachers are compelled, year in and year out, to devote the whole of their time to classes. Even the best of them tire of this unending circle and must in time grow hardened. *Art, in fact, is not a branch of science which can be learned step by step from a book.* Innate artistic ability can only be intensified by influencing the whole being, by the example of the design master and his work. Whereas the technical and scientific subjects can be learned by progressive courses of lectures, the training in design must, to be successful, be conducted as freely as possible, at the personal discretion of the artist. The lessons which are intended to give direction and artistic incentive to the work of the individuals and groups need by no means be very frequent, but they must provide essentials which stimulate the student. The ability to draw is all too frequently confused with the ability to produce creative design. Like dexterity in handicrafts, it is, however, no more than a skill, a valuable means of expressing spatial ideas. Virtuosity in drawing and handicrafts is not art. The artistic training must provide food for the imagination and the creative powers. An intensive 'atmosphere' is the most valuable thing a student can receive. Such a *'fluidum'* can only grow when a number of personalities are working together to a common

C

projects his imagination into the scene, transforming it into a sensational picture giving brilliance, intensity and meaning to the pattern of life before his eyes.

REALITY AND ILLUSION. I remembered this experience when I read a study by Earl C. Kelley of Wayne University about 'education for what is real,' as verified by recent experiments in sensation, made in co-operation with the Dartmouth Eye Institute in Hanover, New Hampshire. One of the basic statements of this remarkable study is:

'We do not get our sensations from things around us but the sensations come from us. Since they do not come from the immediate environment (the present) and obviously cannot come from the future, they come from the past. If they come from the past they must be based on experience.

The demonstration is as follows: You are presented with three peepholes about the size of the pupil of the eye. You are asked to look through these holes in turn. The material back of the holes is well lighted. In each case you see a cube, with its three dimensions and its square sides. In general, the three cubes look substantially the same. All appear to be about the same distance away [*Fig.1*].

Then you are permitted to look back of the boards through which the peepholes run. When you do this, you see that one of the holes indeed has a wire cube back of it. Another, however, has a drawing on a plane, with scarcely any of the lines running parallel. The third is a number of strings stretched between wires running away from the eye.

Neither of the latter two look anything at all like a cube when viewed from behind the scenes. And yet the sensation in each case was a cube. . . .

Widely different materials caused the same pattern on the retina of our eye and resulted in the same sensation. The sensation could not come from the material, since in two cases it was not a cube. It could not come from the pattern on the retina since that pattern was not a cube. The cube does not exist except as we call it a cube; and that sensation did not come from the material in our environment, but from us. It came from prior experience.'

Similarly a baby in the cradle, seeing the moon for the first time in his life, tries to catch it ; *what is at first a mere reflected image on the retina assumes, in later life, symbolic meaning by experience.* But we need not go back to the undeveloped mind of the baby.

SUBCONSCIOUS REACTIONS. For instance when you drive in a car on a slushy road and a passing car coming in the opposite direction hurls slush at your windscreen you blink and dodge. The subconscious reactions are automatic; though our intellect tells us that the windscreen protects us, the reaction to ward off possible danger for our eye re-occurs every time. Our eye obviously does not take any chances.

Imagine sitting on a balcony twenty storeys high above the ground, the balcony having an open railing made of vertical bars. Though the railing gives you physical protection, you will have a sense of giddiness if you look down. Giddiness, however, stops immediately if the railing is covered with cardboard or paper, for this enclosure then gives support to the eye. Our equilibrium is re-established through the illusion of safety although nothing has been added in fact for greater physical safety. The eye does not know, it reacts automatically.

The equivalent phenomenon in horizontal direction is the so-called agoraphobia, i.e., the dread of open spaces which seizes sensitive persons crossing a large open square (*Fig.* 2). They feel lost in a space the size of which is not in keeping with the human scale. But if some vertical planes were erected on that open space like wings on a stage, such as shrubs or fences or walls, the illusion of safety would be reinstated, and the dread would disappear; for the eyes of the person groping in space now find a frame of reference to support them; when they hit a solid in the field of vision they register its outline just as radar does.

These examples show that there is a split between physical perception on the one hand and our intellectual knowledge upper picture you see that the flattening out of the lens brings the sharp adjustment of the image, whereas the lower is blurred because of wrong adjustment. Technology uses the same method for reproducing and printing pictures as nature does in our eye, using a sieve or screen.

In the eye the image projected upon the retina by the lens is likewise broken up into dots by the rods and cones of the retina since each cell sees only one dot no larger than itself. Strongly stimulated cells report to the brain 'light,' weakly stimulated cells 'dark.' If a retinal image were to be magnified several hundred times, we would see that it consists of points or dots just like an enlarged piece of a halftone engraving.

(*Fig. 10*) This is the television apparatus of the human eye which like that of a broadcasting station transforms optical images into electrical currents (a,b,c), the supporting framework (g, h), the photosensitive cells (f), the connecting cells (e), the large transmitting cells (d), the nerve cable (i,k), the protecting base.

(*Fig. 11*) The human eye is a combination camera for day and night photography. The retinal cones on the left are daylight apparatus. They require much light, producing sharply defined panchromatic pictures. The rods in our eye shown on the right side are twilight apparatus. They are strongly photosensitive but produce indistinct achromatic pictures.

The curvature of the retina as well as of our eye lens is the source of certain distortions of images. This complicates further the necessary association of our space-perceiving senses and is the common cause of a wealth of optical illusions. The knowledge of these illusions appears to be indispensable for a designer.

OPTICAL ILLUSIONS. The plainly recognisable concavities of a moon landscape (*Fig.* 12) will appear convex if we turn the picture upside down (*Fig. 13*). Note that the stream running through a valley in the original picture now runs over a crest. Our eyesight is unable to adjust this illusionary phenomenon of reciprocation to the reality of the original view now reversed. Modern abstract painters have made use of the intriguing interplay of form elements which can be read as being either convex or concave, thus giving an illusion of motion.

An accurate square, striped by parallel lines running either horizontally or vertically, appears to be elongated in the opposite direction from that of the parallel lines (*Fig 14*). This is an important fact to know for architectural and fashion design. In addition, the width of the stripes has to be carefully chosen to be in keeping with the size of the figure. The girl in the bathing suit (*Fig. 15*) looks more slender in horizontal than vertical stripes. In the same way the columns of the cathedral of Siena, Italy, (*Fig. 16*) would appear heavier if the stripes were vertical.

Another optical phenomenon is that called 'irradiation.' A bright figure on dark background appears to be larger than a black figure on a bright background (*Fig. 17*). This illusion is caused by the light spilling over the dark edges of a silhouette projected on our retina. Silhouettes of sculptured figures standing against the bright sky appear to be reduced by irradiation. The volume of such sculpture has to be exaggerated in order to give the intended effect of truthfulness (*Fig. 18*). The light nibbles at the contours.

PSYCHOLOGICAL INFLUENCE OF SHAPES AND COLOURS. El Greco's 'Grand Inquisitor' is more than the portrait of a man. It depicts the state of mind this man evoked in the beholder and in the artist. The explosive stroke of the brush and the shapes chosen suggest horror and dread of a terrifying menace—the Inquisition (*Fig. 19*).

Shapes can be exciting or soothing. In addition, their colours —shrill or soft—can increase the intended effect. Colour and texture of surfaces have an effective existence of their own, sending out physical energies which can be measured. Such effect can be warm or cold, advancing or receding, bright or dark, light or heavy, in tension or in suspension, or even attractive or repulsive (*Fig. 20*). A New York designer who calls himself a colour engineer reports that :

'he is sure that violet induces melancholy ; that yellow is an energising colour, conducive to conviviality, increased signer; he also must anticipate the varying distances from which the beholder may view his work. The effect of a building will be intense only when all requirements for human scale have been fulfilled for any potential distance or direction of view.

From far away its silhouette should be simple so that it can be grasped at a glance like a symbol even by an ever so primitive spectator as well as by a man passing in an automobile (*Fig. 25*). When we come closer we distinguish protruding and receding parts of the building, and their shadows serve as scale regulators for the new distance. And finally, standing close by, no longer able to see the whole edifice, the eye should be attracted by a new surprise in the form of refined surface treatment (*Fig. 26*).

Is it the result of instinctive sureness if the designer has applied the proper human scale, or that of knowledge, or does a balance of both account for it?

We know that the Indian architects first had to learn several crafts; then, in their forties, before they were permitted to build a temple, priests gave them secret training in mathematics. I wonder whether they had a science of vision. They certainly did not shrink from complicated working processes in order to achieve a desired optical effect. For instance, the mitre lines of their richly molded cornices do not simply run parallel, as in Western architecture, but they meet in a distant vanishing point. This tapering off creates an optical illusion of greater depth and more impressive scale (*Fig. 27*).

For the same reasons, Iktinos, the designer of the Parthenon, which represents the culmination of perfection and subtlety in Western design, inclined its columns slightly towards the centre axis of the building and delicately curved all its horizontal lines to compensate for the optical illusion of concavity; for a long, straight and horizontal line appears to cave in at its centre because of the curvature of our retina. This distorts and weakens the effect. In order to counteract this illusion, the plinth of the Parthenon was raised four inches higher at its centre than at its ends (*Fig. 28*). It is evident that the base was purposely built this way, for it stands on solid rock and its vertical joints are still very tight today, no settling could have displaced its original lines. Here intuition and intellect joined to triumph over the natural deficiences of human vision. Here is true architecture.

These selected examples characterise the elements which form the language of design. What do we know about the relations of these elements in 'space'? Every one of us has once in his life attempted to understand the infinite space by lying on his back, looking into the stars, thinking and trying to envisage the endlessness of the heavens, only to recognise that we are denied cognition of the infinite. The mathematician has invented the infinitely small and the infinitely large quantity. He has certain signs for them. But each is an abstraction we cannot understand. We comprehend space and scale only within a frame of reference which is finite. Confined space—open or enclosed—is the medium of architecture. The right relation between the building masses and the voids which they enclose is essential in architecture. This may appear obvious, but I have found that many people are not at all conscious of this relation, and that there are even trained architects who design only in terms of the buildings themselves, ignorant of the fact that the open spaces between them are just as important a part of the architectural composition.

Many of us still live innocently in a static three-dimensional world of Newtonian conception which has long since collapsed. Philosophers and scientists have replaced that static conception by a dynamic picture of relativity. In today's design terminology this profound change has been acknowledged by what we call 'space-time' relations. Science has discovered the relativity of all human values and that they are in constant flux. There is no such thing as finality or eternal truth according to science. Transformation is the essence of life. I would like to quote a report about the Princeton Bicentennial meeting, 'Planning Man's Physical Environment':

'The Physical Environment which the architects were invited to consider had changed at a terrorising velocity within their working lifetime. The expanding universe had become the exploding universe, and time, the new Fourth Dimension, had become more ponderable than any of the other sunlight to be used at will, varying in quantity, intensity and colour. However, as long as artificial light cannot yet fully comply with our requirements, I believe that we should not exclude the dynamic qualities of daylight as supplement to artificial lighting wherever it is feasible because it satisfies our need for change. To give you an example of the psychological means at our disposal to keep our senses alert and responsive I shall try to analyse what could be done to make a visit to a museum into a stimulating instead of an exhausting experience. As we know, the capacity of a visitor to receive the messages of many masterpieces, crowded together, will dwindle rapidly unless we are able to refresh him frequently. His mind must be neutralised after each impression before a new impression can sink in. We cannot keep him in a high pitch of ecstacy for hours while he is wandering through a gallery, but the acuity of his interest can be kept awake by skilful design offering him ever varying space and light effects and an arrangement of display that is rich in contrasts. Only if he is thus compelled to use his natural functions of adaptation from tension to repose will he remain an untired and active participant. The arrangement of the exhibition spaces themselves and the distribution of exhibits in them should create a sequence of arresting surprises which must be well timed and properly scaled to fit the visitor's susceptibility. With this demand we enter the realm of architectural creation.

It is evident that motion in space, or the illusion of motion in space produced by the artist's magic, is becoming an increasingly powerful stimulant in contemporary works of architecture, sculpture, painting and design. In architecture today there is a preference for transparency, achieved through large areas of glass and through undercutting and opening parts of the building. This transparency aims at producing the illusion of a floating continuity of space. The buildings seem to hover, space seems to move in and out (*Fig.* 32). Sections of the infinite outdoor space become part of an architectural space composition which does not stop at the enclosing walls, as in past periods, but is carried beyond the building into its surroundings. Space seems to be in motion (*Fig.* 33).

FIG. 31

FIG. 32 : Corner of the Bauhaus building

FIG. 33 : Living room of House Poissy by Le Corbusier

FIG. 34 : Diagram of the Modulor by Le Corbusier

COMMON DENOMINATOR FOR DESIGN. Educat-
ors in design have started to bring new order into the findings
of philosophy and science. A basic philosophy of design needs
first of all a denominator common to all. Some of the initial
groundwork in the formulation of a language of design has
been done by the Bauhaus, by Le Corbusier and Ozenfant in
L'Esprit nouveau, by Moholy-Nagy in his *The New Vision* and
Vision in Motion, by the teachings of Josef Albers, by Kepes's
Language of Vision, by Herbert Read's *Education Through Art*
and particularly by Le Corbusier's *Modulor* (*Fig. 34*) and by
others in these and related fields.

Will we succeed in establishing an optical 'key,' used and
understood by all, as an objective common denominator of
design? This can, of course, never become a recipe or a sub-
stitute for art. *Intellectual art is sterile, and no work of art
can be greater than its creator. The intuitive directness, the
short cut of the brilliant mind, is ever needed to create profound art. But an optical key would provide the impersonal
basis as a prerequisite for general understanding and would
serve as the controlling agent within the creative act.*

Blueprint of an Architect's Education[*]

A. GENERAL EDUCATIONAL BACKGROUND

I believe that every healthy human being is capable of conceiving form. The problem seems to me not at all one of existence of creative ability but more one of finding the key to release it.

This problem is not America's problem alone; but it is perhaps more acute in this country because Americans, in their great enthusiasm for learning, are likely even to outdo Europeans in their efforts to cultivate their receptive and reproductive abilities to such a degree that creative instincts sometimes become submerged. This is not true with respect to the creative and inventive spirit in the technical field. Here the living generation seems to have no difficulty at all in encouraging bold pioneering and proud disregard of standards set by the past. But people behave altogether differently in their attitude toward the arts. Our great heritage seems to have left us stunned and bereft of original impulse and, from being participators and creators, we have changed into connoisseurs and scholars. If we investigate the vague feelings of the average man toward the arts, we find that he is timid and that he has developed a humble belief that art is something which has been invented centuries ago in countries like Greece or Italy and that all we can do about it is to study it carefully and apply it. There is no natural, eager response to the works of modern artists who try to solve contemporary problems in a contemporary way, but, rather, a great uneasiness and a strong disbelief that they can turn out something worthy of the great works of their forefathers.

[*] See : 'Training the Architect' by W. Gropius, *Twice A Year*, Number 2, 1939, New York, *'Plan pour un enseignement de l'Architecture'* by W. Gropius, *L'Architecture d'Aujourd'hui*, Paris, February, 1950.

This surprising sterility is in my opinion due not so much to inborn lack of ability or interest, but is a result of the fact that we are today separated into two groups of beings—the 'public' and the 'expert.' Each person feels that he is an 'expert' in one or two fields and just the 'public' in all the others. But you know, probably, from experience that no one is able really to appreciate any display of ability in any field if he, himself, has not to a certain degree taken part in its problems and difficulties at some time. But the way art and design are taught today to the average youngster often does not give him any clue toward contemporary problems and contemporary tasks. He emerges from school and college filled to the brim with knowledge, but he has rarely been engaged in the task of meeting himself. I think we have been exceedingly successful so far in working out ways of acquainting our children with the achievements of the past, but I do not think we are as successful in stimulating them to come forth with their own ideas. We have made them study art history so hard that they have found no time to express their own ideas. By the time they have grown up they have developed such fixed ideas of what art is that they have ceased to think of it as something to be freely approached and recreated by themselves. They have lost the joyful, playful urge of their early youth to shape things into new forms and have become, instead, self-conscious onlookers. This, however, is not the fault of the individual but seems to have been caused by the social changes in life.

THE ORIGIN OF ABSTRACT ART. When, in the great art periods of former times—say, in the Middle Ages— an artist painted a Madonna, he was immediately understood by everybody on acount of the common, established social and religious background of his contemporaries. Today we are living between two civilisations : the old one went to pieces, the new one is just in the making. An artist of today can be understood only by a clique, not yet by the whole community, as the spiritual content of our civilisation is not yet so firmly settled that it may be clearly symbolised by the artist. This may give us also a clue to what brought about the so-called 'abstract art' of today whose discoveries have so deeply influenced architecture. The community, being deprived of the old standards of social and religious ideals, confined the artist to isolation. He lost touch with the life of the community. His way out of this dilemma was his attempt to concentrate on the very medium of his art, observing and discovering new phenomena in space and colour, and abstaining from any literary content in his work. Naturally, art became severed from the life of the people. That is what we have to face today.

BALANCE BETWEEN EXPERIENCE AND BOOK KNOWLEDGE. I am convinced, though, that in every human being there are artistic faculties; the deeper values of life, however, are being impaired today by putting the emphasis of our existence on secondary considerations: business as an end in itself and this or that practical occupation. The 'trade-mentality,' so to speak, has superseded the desire for a balanced life as it informed former periods. Our whole system of education is directed to fit the man as soon as possible for specialised work. As soon as the happy playtime of the child is over he becomes confined to only one sector of life, losing more and more his innate connection with the totality of life. Discrepancy between occupation and vocation is seriously increasing. The courage to venture into other fields of human experience has vanished in our specialised system of production with its almost exclusively material aims. No doubt education has suffered considerably from our overestimation of material aspects and of a one-sided intellectual approach. Good education, aiming at preparing the individual for a creative attitude and for equipoise in life, must certainly lead him beyond mere fact information and book knowledge into direct personal experience and action. We must give our young people more opportunity to acquire such personal experience during their educational training, for only if we make them 'find' facts by themselves can knowledge turn into wisdom.

It is characteristic of the current trend that most influential educational plans published in recent years treat the visual arts rather casually, not at all as a discipline belonging to the central core of education. *We seem to have forgotten that, since time immemorial, creative aesthetic disciplines in the arts have always generated ethic qualities. We are too overconfident of the benefits from intellectual training. Art, being the product of human desire and inspiration, transcends the realms of logic and reason. It is a field of interest common to all, as beauty is a basic requirement for civilised life.*

The true aim of all education—too often forgotten, however—is to stimulate enthusiasm toward greater effort. I am convinced that 'safety first' is a foul slogan for a young man. The idea of personal security, being in itself an illusion, breeds irresponsibility and egoism. It is a mere materialistic conception. *No durable result in any trend of education can be expected without a dominating ideal, the human or social component of which has to direct the professional one—not vice versa.* Although such an aim may appear self-evident, it has become extremely rare in today's educational practice. Surely a student must be fitted for practical life, but the opposite danger of educating dreamers, secluded from the world, is hardly imminent today. The over-emphasis on fact-knowledge, on intellectual reasoning has obviously carried our generation astray. It has lost touch with the totality of life and with its social implications. Intuitive quality—eternal source of all creative action—is being underrated. We see our youth mistrusting their own instincts and denying everything which cannot be conclusively reasoned. In my opinion they should, instead, be encouraged to be heedful of their emotions, learning to control rather than to subdue them. They need spiritual guidance beyond professional practicalities to develop their own creative substance, not only their intellect. The greater the spiritual aims, the better youth will conquer material difficulties. *When intuition has found food, skill develops most rapidly while routine alone can never supersede creative vision. Highest reality can be given shape only by a being who has comprehended sublimest unreality.*

METHOD OF TEACHING. For this part of his training consistency of approach in his studies is imperative. Overwhelmed by the profusion of contradictory opinions about the world at large as they are offered by institutions of higher learning he is in danger of becoming apathetic or cynical unless his educators present him with a very definite and, as it were, unilateral curriculum which should not change its direction until a certain maturity is reached and a conviction has been formed. The objection that such a consistent method would be too one-sided is not valid, for only he who has understood really well one way of thinking will be able later to compare it to other ways of thinking and to select elements from them intelligently for his own creative attempts.

The teaching of a method of approach is more important than the teaching of skills. It should be a continuing process which must grow concentrically like the annual rings of a tree. In all its stages the scope should be all-embracing instead of sectional, increasing slowly in intensity and detail in all fields of discipline simultaneously. The integration of the whole range of knowledge and experience is of the greatest importance right from the start; only then will the totality of aspect make sense in the student's mind. He will easily absorb all further details and place them where they belong if he progresses from the whole to the details, and not vice versa.

Such an educational approach would start the student off into a creative effort toward integrating simultaneously design, construction and economy of any given task with its social ends. Obvious as this demand appears to be from an intellectual point of view, educational experience has shown that it takes years to bring the student into the habit of simultaneously conceiving all three—design, construction and economy—as an inseparable and interdependent entity. The reason for the widespread sectional approach in architectural education seems to be the over-emphasis on intellectual academic training and the resulting lack of opportunity for experience in field and workshop. I cannot see why knowledge alone should be made the primary object of education, when direct experience is just as indispensable as a basis for subsequent training. Paper has become too exclusive a medium of exchange. The book and the draughting board cannot give that invaluable experience gained by trial and error in the workshop and on the building site. Such experience should therefore be interwoven into the training right from the start, not added on later, after the academic part of learning has been already completed. For practical experience is the best means of guaranteeing a synthesis of all the emotional and intellectual factors in the student's mind; it prevents him from rushing off into 'precocious' design, not sufficiently weighted down by the know-how of the building process. No doubt the fatal separation between craftsmanship and academic learning during the development of the machine age has split architecture from building. The problem of how to co-ordinate both—scientific knowledge and field experience—is crucial in our educational system. I will try to outline, therefore, a plan which might help to correct these present deficiences, starting off first with a suggestion for a more scientific approach in design.

The general indolence of people toward the arts and architecture and the prevalent methods of education in design seem to be interdependent. Through improved education people should be encouraged to believe again in the basic importance of art and architecture for their daily lives. But so long as we consider the problems involved to be a matter of individual feelings which cannot be objectively defined to standards of value, we cannot expect them to be recognised as basic for educational progress. *The spiritual implications of art in society are to be redefined and, with the help of the scientists and using their methods of precision, the social and psychological components of art—not only the technical ones—are to be determined by a distinct order of values and meanings.*

COMMON DENOMINATOR OF DESIGN. Basic order in design needs first of all a denominator common to all, derived from facts. A common language of visual communication will give the designer a foundation of solidarity for his spontaneous expression in art; it will free him from the sad isolation from which he is suffering at present since, in a socially disrupted world, we have lost the common key for understanding the visual arts.

In music a composer still uses a musical key to make his composition understood. Within the framework of only twelve notes the greatest music has been created. Limitation obviously makes the creative mind inventive.

In architecture the 'golden means,' the 'modules' of the Greeks, the 'triangulation' of the Gothic builders give evidence that in the past also optical keys have existed, serving as common denominators for the working teams of early builders.

For a long period, however, no common denominator has guided our expression in the visual arts. But today, after a long, chaotic period of *'l'art pour l'art,'* a new language of vision is slowly replacing individualistic terms like 'taste' or 'feeling' with terms of objective validity. Based on biological facts—both physical and psychological—it seeks to represent the impersonal cumulative experience of successive generations. Here roots true tradition.

LANGUAGE OF VISION. In modern architecture and design there is a reawakening toward a language of vision. We are able today to feed the creative instinct of a designer with richer knowledge of visual facts, such as the phenomena of optical illusion, of the relation of solids and voids in space, of light and shade, of colour and of scale; objective facts instead of arbitrary, subjective interpretation or formulas long since stale.

Order of course can never become a recipe for making art. The artist's inspirational spark transcends logic and reason. But a language of vision derived from old and new discoveries in science controls his creative act. It provides simultaneously the common key for understanding the artist's message and transforms its paradoxical content into visible terms of expression.

Yet before it can become common to all, it must be made valid through general education. This goal cannot be reached by theoretical knowledge alone; it must be combined with continuous practical experience.

EMPHASIS ON PRACTICAL EXPERIENCE. Emotional faculties cannot be trained by analytical methods but only by creative disciplines as in music, poetry and the visual arts. Making is certainly not a mere auxiliary to thinking. It is a basic experience indispensable for the unity of purpose within the creative act. It is the only educational means which interrelates our perceptive and inventive faculties.

If we compare teaching the arts of design in the past with our present methods of training, the discrepancy becomes apparent at a glance. In the past, design was developed from apprenticeship in workshops—today, from the platonic draughting board. What used to be an auxiliary only for the maker of things—paper design—has become the central discipline of the designer. This shift of emphasis from learning by doing to intellectual discipline is typical of the present educational methods in design. But can an architect become a master of his craft without previous experience with tools and materials, without the know-how of an illuminating experience in building and making? Should architectural education then be separated from its present academic framework? Many architects would agree with a decisive turn toward greater emphasis on practical experience. I, personally, have grave doubts as to whether the present bookish climate of universities can offer at all a healthy breeding ground for architects. The impact of industrialisation on our profession has been so decisive that the young generation of designers should be trained in close touch with the building industries and with their laboratories. As such a desirable change develops slowly, however, I shall attempt here to outline a transitional curriculum which, making use of existing academic facilities, aims at balancing academic learning by direct experiences in the workshop and on the building site.

EXPERIMENTAL WORKSHOP AND PRELIMINARY DESIGN COURSE. A continuous training of basic manual skill in experimental workshops combined with disciplines in the fundamentals of surface, volume and space, and of composition—derived from objective findings—must be developed on all levels of general and professional education. Both the reinstatement of workshop practice and the introduction of scientific courses leading to a common language of visual communication are basic requirements for successful teaching of the arts of design and especially of architecture.

This training should start with a general preliminary course aimed at co-ordinating the elements of handwork and design. As the beginner does not yet know the relationship in which he stands to the world at large, it would be wrong to put the 'trade' idea or any specialisation at the beginning of his training. *In his natural readiness to grasp life as a whole a student should first get a comprehensive view of the vast field of possibilities for expression lying before him.* The customary training in mere drawing is not sufficient as a preparation. Drawing and painting are certainly most valuable means of self-expression, but paper, pencil, brush and water colour are not enough to develop the sense of space so necessary to freedom of expression. The student should be introduced first, therefore to three-dimensional experiments; that is, to the elements of ' building,' i.e., composition in space with all sorts of experiments in materials. For example, observing the contrast between rough and smooth, hard and soft, tension and repose, will help the student to discover for himself by exercise of his hands the pecularities of materials, their structure and textures. Working with materials, the student begins simultaneously to understand surface, volume, space and colour. In addition to technical skill, he develops his own form language in order to be able to give visible expression to his ideas. After he has absorbed the elementary studies, he should then be ready to attempt compositions of his own invention.

The aim of such design work is to widen the personality rather than to provide professional skill. Its success will depend greatly on the qualities of the teacher who, by encouraging and stimulating, must release the student's own imagination, must oppose with objectivity any reproduction or imitation of other people's conceptions, including his own. The student will then experience his own ability for making creative short cuts which go beyond his preceding intellectual research.

Such a training will give confidence and independence and will thus enhance the productiveness and speed of any subsequent professional training.

PROFESSIONAL TRAINING. After such preliminary experience the professional designer can then start his specialised curriculum from solid ground. Still he will need the workshop and the building site all along, to relate his design to the realities of materials and techniques. It is then that he will realise that his knowledge of the language of vision, his skill in construction, in draftsmanship and representation are all indispensable implements for expressing the all-important social end of his creative effort.

FIELD PRACTICE. In educational practice, the best means of preserving the unity of the entire training on all levels is to relate it to as many realistic experiences as possible. The problems given should be built up on real conditions, suggesting an actual site and calling in a 'client.' The more the collaboration between teachers and students resembles office practice, the better. Visiting buildings under construction, manufacturing plants, research institutes will stimulate the student's imagination and strengthen his understanding of making and building. But most important, he should work as an apprentice on a building under construction or as an assistant to its clerk-of-the-works, in order to learn to cope with the elements of the building process, the assembly of building parts and the potential frictions between the various subcontractors. How can a student understand flashing and roofing via the drafting board, or the economical and technical problems involved in the sequence of the building process merely from drawings? In practice only, closely observing the procedure of executing a building from drawings, will he gather experience which will make sense to him. Knowledge collected by others and handed out to him theoretically remains a contention without proof in his mind; he can learn by experience only and not by authority. Every student, before applying for a professional degree, should therefore see a building being constructed from start to finish ; such experience should be made obligatory.

In addition to such field practice, graduate schools should run a laboratory workshop in connection with a sample collection. Here, experiments should be made by teachers and

students together for the finish of interior and exterior parts
of buildings—textures and colours—and of their relations in
space. As the practical part of the architect's profession is
highly technical, he should be given opportunities for experimenting and testing similar to those given to students of
medicine, biology and chemistry in their laboratories.

HISTORY   OF   ART   AND   ARCHITECTURE.
Studies in the history of art and architecture, intellectual and
analytical in character, make the student familiar with the
conditions and reasons which have brought about the visual
expression of the different periods: i.e., the changes in
philosophy, in politics and in means of production caused by
new inventions. Such studies can verify principles found by
the student through his own previous exercises in surface,
volume, space and colour; they cannot by themselves, however,
develop a code of principles to be valid for present creation
in design. Principles have to be established for each period
from new creative work. History studies are therefore best
offered to older students who have already found self-
expression. When the innocent beginner is introduced to the
great achievements of the past, he may be too easily discour-
aged from trying to create for himself. As soon as he has
found his bearings, however, through self-expression in workshop and studio, history studies are a welcome means of
refining his thinking without luring him into an imitative
attitude. These studies should be started in the third year,
instead of in the first year of training.

I sum up my conclusions for a transitional approach in
architectural education :

1. The architect is to be a co-ordinator—a man of vision
and professional competence—whose business it is to unify
the many social, technical, economic and artistic problems
which arise in connection with building.

The architect has to recognise the impact of industrialisation
and should explore the new relationships dictated by the
social and scientific progress.

2. In an age of specialisation, method is more important
than information. The training of an architect should be

concentric rather than sectional. In essence it should be all-inclusive throughout its duration, gaining in certainty of approach—that is, in clearness of thought and in the know-how of its realisation. It should aim at teaching the student that it is through a creative attitude and independence of conception that he will arrive at basic convictions, not by accepting ready-made formulas.

Most essential is the unity of educational purpose. Man is to be the focus; his spiritual and material needs in relation to the life of the community should determine all stages of the student's training.

2a.   The approach toward any kind of design—of a chair, a building, a whole town or a regional plan—should be essentially identical not only in respect to their relationship in space but to social aspects as well. The common ideal to which all are addressed should be emphasised above their material and technical means of realisation; for all products of design are to be part of the organic whole, part of our man-made environment in town and country.

3.   Three-dimensional conception is the basic architectural discipline. Methods of stimulating interest in visual expression in all fields of the plastic arts must train the student first to see, to perceive distance, and to grasp the human scale. Such disciplines are indispensable for acquiring the instinctive sureness to organise three-dimensional space and to conceive it simultaneously in terms of structural efficiency, economy of means and harmony of appearance.

4.   Knowledge will come to life only by individual experience. Therefore, designing and building—the drafting board and the job—should be closely related on all levels. Field practice should not be added on as a separate experience, after an academic training of several years' duration has been completed. It should be an integral part of the curriculum itself.

5.   In the first year, basic design-and-workshop practice combined should introduce to the students the elements of construction and of 'building' by developing three-dimensional exercises to be carried out with materials and tools. At the same time a design course, incorporating actual problems,

should focus all activities of the group on the social aim of improving the life of the community. Elements of planning are to be included in these comprehensive initial studies.

6. In the second and third year, the design-and-construction studio, supplemented by field experience during the summer vacations and by activities in a laboratory, will correlate further experience with the broadening knowledge. The term 'field experience' does not refer to work in an office, but to practice directly in the field, as an assistant to the foreman or the supervisor. This field experience—not less than six months—should be made obligatory for any professional degree in architecture. It should include also acquaintance with the building industry.

7. Construction should be taught as part and parcel of design, for both are directly interdependent. Equal emphasis must be put on both; no student should be promoted so long as he is deficient in either one. Design and construction problems should be related to actual conditions regarding the site and the requirements for the use of the building. They should be approached as inseparable from the problems of the community which include the all important factors of economy.

8. The students should be trained to work in teams—also with students of related techniques—in order to learn methods of collaboration with others. This will prepare them for their vital task of becoming co-ordinators of the many individuals involved in the conception and execution of planning and building projects. The nature of teamwork will lead the students to good well-co-ordinated architecture rather than to flashy 'stunt' design.

9. History studies should be started in the third year rather than in the first, to avoid intimidation and imitation. They should help the maturer students to analyse the origin of masterworks of the past and to show him how the architectural conception of a past period, as evident from the remaining examples, resulted from its religion, its social set up and its means of production.

10. Teachers should be appointed only after sufficient practical experience of their own, both in design and building. The trend to engage young men as teachers who have just

1906 : Sullivan

FIG. 35 : Originators of the new architecture up to 1914

1910 : Behrens

1910 : Loos

1911 : Gropius

1911-1913 : Perret

1911 : Poelz

1914 : Berlag

1913 : St. Elia

completed an academic training is harmful. For only teachers with broad experience can muster the desirable resourcefulness so necessary to stimulate the student consistently all along. The best education can offer is stimulation, for it makes the student eager to use his own initiative. Every teacher in architecture and engineering should have the right to private practice, for this alone can replenish his resourcefulness. Without such opportunity, he is bound to dry out rapidly and then withdraw to an 'authoritative' platform.

11. Schools of architecture of smaller size—say, with an enrolment of 100 or 150 students—are more efficient than large ones. The most valuable intangible of a school, an intensive 'atmosphere,' results from mutual participation of faculty and students in all activities ; this is easily lost in over-sized schools so adverse to intimate group effort.

12. The efficiency of teaching performance depends on the number of students per teacher. An architect's training calls for individual coaching in order to help the student on terms adapted to his own personal talent and state of development. An overburdened teacher will be lost to all of his students. The desirable number of students per teacher should be twelve to sixteen at the most.

The emphasis in all my arguments is on the creative factor. That is, that a programme of search rather than research makes the creative architect. Such a programme, I believe, will lead our potential architects from observation to discovery to invention and finally to an intuitive shaping of our contemporary scene.

E

II

The Contemporary Architect

Appraisal of the Development of.
Modern Architecture*

Today we are in a position to prove conclusively that the out-
ward forms of modern architecture are not the whim of a few
architects hungry for innovation, but the inevitable conse-
quential product of the intellectual, social and technical conditions of our age. It has taken a quarter of a century of earnest
and pregnant struggle to bring these forms into being—forms
which evince so many fundamental structural changes when
compared with those of the past. I think the present situation
can be summed up as follows : a breach has been made with
the past which enables us to envisage a new aspect of architecture corresponding to the technical civilisation of the age
we live in; the morphology of dead styles has been destroyed
and we are returning to honesty of thought and feeling; the
general public, which was formerly indifferent to everything
to do with building, has been shaken out of its torpor; personal
interest in architecture as something that concerns every one
of us in our daily lives has been aroused in wide circles; and
the lines of future development have become clearly manifest
throughout Europe.

But this development has encountered obstacles: confusing
theories, dogmas and personal manifestoes; technical difficulties and finally the dangers arising from formalistic will-o'-the-
wisps. The worst of all of these was that modern architecture
became fashionable in several countries! Imitation, snobbery
and mediocrity have distorted the fundamentals of truth and
simplicity on which this renaissance was based. Spurious
phrases like 'functionalism' and 'fitness for purpose equals

* See : 'The Formal and Technical Problems of Modern Architecture
and Planning' by W. Gropius, *Journal of the Royal Institute of British
Architects*, London, May 19, 1934.

beauty' have deflected appreciation of the new architecture into minor and purely external channels. This one-sided characterisation is reflected in that frequent ignorance of the true motives of its founders, and a fatal obsession which impels superficial people to try to relegate this phenomenon to one isolated province instead of perceiving that it is a bridge which unites opposite poles of thought.

The idea of rationalisation, which many people aver is the outstanding characteristic of the new architecture, is only its purifying role. The other aspect, the satisfaction of the human soul, is just as important as the material. Both find their counterpart in that unity which is life itself. The liberation of architecture from the mass of ornament, the emphasis on the functions of its structural members and the quest for concise and economical solutions, only represent the material side of that formalising process on which the practical value of the new architecture depends. *What is far more important than this structural economy and its functional emphasis is the intellectual achievement which has made possible a new spatial vision—for whereas the practical side of building is a matter of construction and materials, the very nature of architecture makes it dependent on the mastery of space.*

The transformation from manual to machine production so preoccupied humanity for a century that instead of pressing forward to tackle the real problems of design, men were long content with borrowed styles and formalistic decorations.

This state of affairs is over at last. A new conception of building, based on realities, has developed; and with it has come a new and changed perception of space. The very different appearance of the numerous good examples of the new architecture which already exist exemplify these changes and the new technical means we now use to express them.

How far has the struggle progressed in the meantime, and what parts have the various nations played in it? I will begin with the precursors of the pre-war era, and confine myself to contrasting the actual founders of the new architecture up to 1914 : Berlage, Behrens, myself, Poelzig, Loos, Perret, Sullivan and St. Elia; and drawing up a brief balance of their joint achievement. The governing factors in my choice will be, not the aesthetics of the buildings concerned, but the degree of independence and creative achievement with which in these buildings their architects have definitely enriched the movement. With one exception this choice is based not on paper projects, but executed designs: a consideration which seems to me of some importance.

Germany played a leading rôle in the development of the new architecture. Long before the war the Deutscher Werkbund had been formed in Germany. At that time such an outstanding leader as Peter Behrens was not a strange or isolated phenomenon. On the contrary, he already had a powerful backing in the Deutscher Werkbund, a body which formed a reservoir of the forces of progress and renewal. I well remember the animated discussion at the Werkbund's public sessions during the Cologne Exhibition of 1914 which so many foreigners attended; and the publication of the first of the Werkbund's well-known year-books at about the same time. It was in active collaboration in the latter that I gained my first comprehensive insight into the movement as a result of drawing up a sort of inventory of the existing state of architecture. Between 1912 and 1914, too, I designed my first two important buildings : the Fagus Factory at Alfeld, and the Office Building for the Cologne Exhibition, both of which clearly evince that emphasis on function which characterises the new architecture.

During this same pre-war period Auguste Perret was the leading personality in France. The Théâtre des Champs Elysées in Paris, built in 1911-13, was designed by Perret in collaboration with the Belgian Van de Velde, who was then living in Weimar and working in close contact with the Deutcher Werkbund. Perret's chief title to fame is his extraordinary constructive skill, which altogether surpasses his gifts as spatial designer. Although more engineer than architect, he indubitably belongs to the founders of modern architecture, for it was he who succeeded in freeing architecture from its ponderous monumentalism by his audacious and wholly unprecedented forms of construction. Yet this great pioneer for long remained a voice crying in the wilderness as far as France was concerned.

In Austria, Otto Wagner had built his Post Office Savings Headquarters in Vienna at the turn of the century. Wagner dared to expose plain surfaces entirely free of decoration and mouldings. Today, it is almost impossible for us to imagine what a revolution such a step implied. Simultaneously Adolph Loos, another Viennese, began writing those articles and books in which he set forth the fundamentals of the new architecture, and building that large shop in the Michaelplatz, immediately opposite the Hofburg in Vienna, which so inflamed the passions of a population accustomed to Baroque forms.

In 1913 Futurism was launched in Italy, of which St. Elia, who unfortunately died in the war, was one of the leading adherents. At the 1933 Triennial Exhibition in Milan his memory was invoked by Marinetti, the founder of Futurism, as one of the great originators of the new architecture. St. Elia wrote astonishingly accurate anticipations of the ideology of the coming architecture, but he never had a chance to carry out any practical work. His project for a skyscraper on a four-tiered street remained a paper design.

In Holland development was slower. Berlage, De Bazel and Lauweriks, who based their work on anthropological premises, had reanimated the use of geometrical systems in design, and had also, in emulation of those important English pioneers, Ruskin and Morris, inspired a revival of handicrafts. A romantic mystical school continued in Holland until well into the post-war decade. It was in 1917, three years after the Cologne Exhibition, that the group known as 'Stijl' was formed, of which Oud and Van Doesburg became the leaders. In 1914 the most advanced buildings in Holland were Berlage's office buildings and De Klerk's housing blocks.

In the United States the revival of architecture had begun as far back as the eighties, simultaneously with the development of a new constructional technique.

Root built a brick skyscraper in Chicago in 1883. About the end of the century Sullivan—Frank Lloyd Wright's far too little recognised master—constructed buildings of this type which are epoch-making, and also formulated architectural principles which contain the pith of the functional doctrines of today. We must not forget that it was Sullivan who wrote,

'Form should follow function.' Intellectually speaking, he was more articulate in his ideas that Frank Lloyd Wright, who was later to inspire so many European architects in both a spatial and a structural sense. Later on, and more particularly in the post-war period, Frank Lloyd Wright began to manifest a growing attachment to romanticism in his lectures and articles that was in sharp contradiction to the European development of the new architecture. At the present moment the Americans have the most fully developed constructional technique of any nation in the world—as I had an opportunity of seeing for myself in the course of my investigations in the United States. But in spite of Sullivan and Frank Lloyd Wright and a very highly developed technical organisation, their artistic evolution has remained in abeyance. The intellectual and cultural background necessary for its preparation does not as yet exist.

This outlines the most important development in the period prior to the war. The war intervened, but at its close the new architecture blossomed forth simultaneously in several centres. The most organic and continuous progress was made in Germany, where leaders of the movement were all moving spirits in the Deutscher Werkbund, and a wide circle of supporters was soon found to share their views. In 1919 the Bauhaus was founded at Weimar, and later on its practical influence on housing developments in the cities with its marked social effect became apparent. Thereafter the movement began to be welcomed by public authorities at large.

In Holland the 'Stijl' movement began to take root; Oud, Rietveld, and Van Loghem built their first buildings, and the City of Amsterdam its extensive housing estates. The 'Stijl' movement had a marked effect as propaganda, but it overemphasised formalistic tendencies, and so provided the impulse that made 'cubic' forms fashionable. The structural concepts of the new architecture are now beginning to oust the theories which inspired the Dutch Modernists.

About the same time, the French-Swiss Corbusier, who had studied for a time under Peter Behrens, began to work in France. In 1916 he was still using pilasters and cornices, but shortly afterward he started to edit *L'Esprit Nouveau*, and to produce architectural and literary work of an astonishingly wide scope which made a profound impression on the young generation in every country. But in contrast to Germany, where a whole following had sprung up in and around the Bauhaus, the movement in France developed only as the purely personal concern of a few individuals; and people in general remained indifferent, with the result that no new school arose as a logical result of their activities.

Switzerland produced a number of capable architects after the war who considerably influenced the movement, more particularly in regard to town planning.

The Stockholm Exhibition of 1930 was an important success for the new architecture in the Scandinavian countries.

England's contribution has been confined to housing and town planning; but Sir Raymond Unwin's ideas and the English garden cities have influenced the whole European housing movement.

Bourgeois accomplished useful pioneering work in Belgium, and has taken a successful part in the replanning of Brussels.

Vigorous young groups have been formed in Czechoslovakia, Poland, Spain and England; while a very active Japanese group exists at Osaka.

In the United States, the Austrian Neutra and the Dane Lönberg-Holm, who have made their home there, and who are both men of outstanding initiative and energy, are carrying on the movement. The younger generation of Americans, some of whom studied at the Bauhaus, are slowly beginning to find their bearings and evolve their own formal components.

The appearance of co-operative working groups, to which I have just drawn attention, is characteristic of the latest development of the new architecture. In countries which might be supposed to have least in common with one another similar free organisations of young architects have been formed, roughly speaking, on the Bauhaus model, who collaborate in practical and experimental work. I consider this co-operative principle particularly promising, and very appropriate to the spirit of our age; especially when these groups include engineers and economists. Such groups—when led by men who possess the right qualifications for holding their members together and inspiring the team spirit—are a guarantee for the thoroughness and many-sidedness of the work produced, as each member inspires his fellow. But groups of this kind must be founded on a voluntary basis. It is impossible to run them within the usual frame of rules and regulations.

An international organisation based on the same principles called 'Les Congrés Internationaux d'Architecture Moderne' (CIAM) was formed in Switzerland ; to which twenty-seven national groups have since adhered. The objects of the congress are to pool the experience of the different countries, and to co-ordinate the results so as to provide practical data and sound directives for town planning and to insure their recognition and adoption in the various countries. This orientation of the congress work is not, of course, accidental, but represents a direct continuation of the original principles of the new architecture applied to the larger unit of the town. The conception which the new kind of architect has of his calling, as that of a co-ordinating organiser, whose business it is to resolve all formal, technical, sociological and commercial problems and combine them in a comprehensive unity, has inevitably extended his researches beyond the house to the street, from the street to the more complete organism which is the city itself ; and ultimately into the wider field of regional and national planning. I believe that the future development of the new architecture is bound to embrace these wider spheres, and concern itself with all their congruent details; and that it must inevitably progress toward an ever fuller conception of the province of design and construction as one vast indivisible whole whose roots are embedded in life itself.

In the face of these proofs of the genuineness of the movement no one who takes the trouble to investigate its sources can possibly still maintain that it is based on an anti-traditional obsession for technique qua technique which blindly seeks to destroy deeper loyalties and is doomed to lead to the deification of pure materialism. The order by which it seeks to restrict arbitrary caprice is the result of a most thorough social, technical and artistic investigation. *I believe that our conception of the new architecture is nowhere in opposition to that of tradition; since respect for tradition does not imply an aesthetic preoccupation with bygone forms of art, but is, and always has been, a struggle for essentials—that is to say, a struggle to get at what is at the back of all technique, which is forever seeking visible expression with its help.*

Archeology or Architecture for
Contemporary Buildings?*

Architecture is said to be a true mirror of the life and social behaviour of a period. If that is true, we should be able to read from its present features the driving forces of our own time. There is conflicting evidence, however. If we compare current public buildings—for example, the 'classical' character of the National Gallery in Washington—with the contemporary character of the new group of buildings for the United Nations, a deep-seated controversy becomes apparent.

We will find an even more puzzling discrepancy if we observe the current state of collegiate architecture, which is bound, of course, to influence the next generation growing up in and around it.

Should it follow the Gothic tradition or the Georgian tradition or should it fulfil the requirements of new college buildings by using 'modern' means of expression unprejudiced by any period design? And, if this last trend seems to have become more prevalent in recent years, why is that so? What is happening to tradition? What stand will finally be taken by responsible educators? These questions seem to touch the very roots of our civilisation, laying open both its weaknesses and its virtues.

Good original architecture depends just as much on an understanding public as on its creators.

Vasari tells the revealing story of Brunelleschi's cathedral in Florence and how the entire population participated in its development. People get the kind of architecture they are ready for, and tendencies in education which foster either

---

* This article, published in the *New York Times Magazine* of October 23, 1949, under the title 'Not Gothic But Modern for Our Colleges,' received the Howard Myers Memorial Prize in 1951.

creative habits or imitative habits are decisive in forming their attitude.

One of the consequences of our purely analytical and intellectual approach to education has been the habit of teaching the visual arts by historical and critical methods of appreciation and information instead of by participation in the processes and techniques of making things. Aesthetic connoisseurship has generally displaced a creative conception of art.

Here, then, we find the very reason for the timid attitude so often shown when the architectural character of new college buildings has to be decided upon. We seem to have forgotten that there is an opportunity to make architectural history for ourselves and to have buildings designed in unmistakable terms of our own period.

What we need is a new code of visual values. So long as we flounder about in a limitless welter of borrowed artistic expression, we shall not succeed in giving form and substance to our own culture, for this implies selective choice of those artistic means which best express the ideas and spiritual directions of our time.

The impact of environment on a young man during his college years is certainly decisive. If the college is to be the cultural breeding ground for the coming generation, its attitude should be creative, not imitative. Stimulating environment is just as important to free the student's creative talent as vigorous teaching.

Accordingly, the student needs the real thing, not buildings in disguise. So long as we do not ask him to go about in period clothes, it seems absurd to build college buildings in pseudo-period design. How can we expect our students to become bold and fearless in thought and action if we encase them timidly in sentimental shrines, feigning a culture which has long since disappeared?

The physical and spiritual functions determining the design of a building are interdependent. They are both part of our present life. It is an anachronism to express the physical functions with the newest technical means but to express the spiritual functions by borrowing a historical shell from the past. Such an attempt confuses the art of architecture with applied archeology. Genuine architecture of organic growth implies continuous renewal.

As history shows, the conception of 'beauty' has changed along with progress in thought and technique. *Whenever man imagined he had found 'eternal beauty,' he fell back into imitation and stagnation. True tradition is the result of constant growth; its quality must be dymanic, not static, to serve as an inexhaustible stimulus to man.*

If, from this vantage point, I now look at my own immediate problem in hand—the design of the new Graduate Centre for Harvard University—and contemplate the way in which these structures can be made into a vital link between the historic mission of a great educational institution and the restless, inquisitive minds of the young men and women of today, I know that it cannot be done without enlisting the student's wholehearted emotional response as well as by paying due respect to the specific architectural tradition of Harvard University.

What now is this tradition? Harvard's 'Yard,' so familiar to many sons of this country, shows a sound basic theme of architectural design which has been reverently kept throughout the centuries by almost all the architects who have contributed individual buildings; a composition of quadrangles, varying in size and confined by individually different buildings, offers a sequence of arresting surprises in space.

This spatial theme fulfils an ancient requirement of the art of architecture—namely, to balance artfully the building masses and open spaces in conformity with the human capacity to experience and sense harmonious space and scale.

The buildings themselves, however, though each is an integral part of the whole, do not 'match.' Harvard's most famous architectural bequests, built during three centuries, could hardly differ more strikingly in their enriching contrasts of forms and colours. Yet they all conform to the noble spatial pattern of the Harvard Yard.

Careful study of this existing pattern of open spaces and structures has therefore become the starting point for the design of the new Harvard Graduate Centre. For here lies the inherent tradition of the Yard; its timeless pattern may well be interpreted again today in new terms of architecture, valid for present-day life.

There is no need to emulate the 'atmosphere' of this or that period. *New buildings must be invented, not copied.* The great periods of architecture in the past have never imitated the periods of their forefathers. In one and the same famous building we can find, side by side, the characteristic shapes of the Romanesque, the Gothic and the Renaissance.

There is no copying to be found in order to preserve an external 'cosmetic' uniformity. Unity was expressed by adherence to the given spatial order of existing buildings, not by imitating their veneers; exterior conformity was never mandatory in the past. Only our aesthetic preoccupation with bygone periods has forced the 'classical' façade on hundreds of college buildings built in the industrial age.

I believe that a different approach is needed which would seek to interpret by a new architectural expression the great changes which have taken place in our time.

For instance, it is a challenging problem in modern architecture to make use of repetitive standard parts, but at the same time to organise these parts in groups which vary in appearance. In the Graduate Centre we strove to break the monotony which might have resulted from repetitive fenestration by changing the direction of the dormitory blocks as well as the design of their ends and links. This has resulted in a variety of different views for the onlooker.

We have also learned that the human being needs frequently changing impressions in order to keep his receptive abilities alert. *To produce such a stimulus for him contemporary artists and architects try to create the illusion of motion.* The confining, cagelike Georgian windows which in their time were necessary due to limitations in the manufacturing of glass have been supplanted by large window openings and undivided glass panes. These permit us to make sections of outdoor space a part of the total architectural composition which does not stop at walls as in the past, but produces the illusion of a continuity of space in motion. This new relationship of interior spaces to the infinite reaches of the outdoors is a characteristic new achievement of modern architecture which consciously or subconsciously must influence everybody's mind.

Building with elements of the handicraft periods in an age of industrialisation is becoming more and more a hopeless task, which either bogs down in financial difficulties because of the paucity of skillful labour needed or ends in a lifeless fake product of industrial origin.

We cannot go on indefinitely reviving revivals. Architecture must move on or die. Its new life must come from the tremendous changes in the social and technical fields during the last two generations.

Neither medievalism nor colonialism can express the life of the twentieth-century man. *There is no finality in architecture —only continuous change.*

The Architect Within Our Industrial Society*

BACKGROUND ANALYSIS. In my analysis I anticipate that architecture as an art starts beyond the demands of construction and economy on the psychological plane of human existence. *The satisfaction of the human psyche resulting from beauty is just as important for a full, civilised life, or even more so, than the fulfilment of our material comfort requirements.* The emotional blocks which bar the development of more organically balanced living must be met at the psychological level, just as our practical problems are met at the technical level.

Is the maker of the rose or the tulip an artist or a technician? Both, for *in nature utility and beauty are constitutional qualities, mutually and truthfully interdependent. The organic form process in nature is the perpetual model for every human creation, whether it results from the mental strife of the inventive scientist or from the intuition of the artist.*

We all still have before our mind that unity of environment and spirit that prevailed in the horse and buggy time. We sense that our own period has lost that unity, that the *sickness of our present chaotic environment, its often pitiful ugliness and disorder have resulted from our failure to put basic human needs above economical and industrial requirements.* Overwhelmed by the miraculous potentialities of the machine human greed has obviously interfered with the biological cycle of human companionship which keeps a community healthy. At the lower level of society the human being has been degraded by being used as an industrial tool. This is the real cause for the fight between capital and labour and for the deterioration

* See: 'Gropius Appraises Today's Architect,' *Architectural Forum*, New York, May, 1952.

of community relations. We now face the difficult task to re-balance the life of the community and to humanise the impact of the machine. It dawns on us that the social component weighs heavier than all the technical, economic and aesthetic problems involved. *The key for a successful rebuilding of our environment—which is the architect's great task—will be our determination to let the human element be the dominant factor.*

But in spite of the effort of quite a few of us, we obviously did not yet find the spiritual bond to hold us together for a concerted effort at establishing a cultural denominator strong enough to becalm our fears and to grow into a common standard of expression.

The artists among us must grow impatient for such a synthesis, which would make whole what is now still unhappily disconnected.

We cannot deny that art and architecture had become an aesthetic end in themselves, because they had lost touch with the community and the people during the industrial revolution. The external embellishments of a building were designed mainly to outdo those of the neighbouring building instead of being developed as a type fit to be used repeatedly as a unit in an organic neighbourhood pattern. The emphasis on being different instead of searching for a common denominator characterised our last generation of architects who dreaded the anti-human influence of the machine. The new philosophy in architecture recognises the predominance of human and social requirements and it accepts the machine as the modern vehicle of form to fulfil these very requirements.

If we look backward into the past we discover the curious fact that a combination of both, a common denominator of form expression and individual variety was in evidence. *The desire to repeat a good standard form seems to be a function of society, and that was true long before the impact of industrialisation.* The designation 'standard' as such has nothing to do with the means of producing it—the hand tool or the machine. Our future houses will not necessarily be regimented because of standardisation and prefabrication; natural competition on the free market will take care of individual variety of the component parts of buildings, just as we experience today a rich diversity of types for machine-made everyday goods on the market. Men did not hesitate to accept widely repeated, standard forms in the pre-machine periods of civilisation. Such standards resulted from their means of production and from their way of living. They represented a combination of the very best many individuals have contributed to the solution of a problem. The standard forms of architecture of the past express a happy blend of technique and imagination, or rather a complete coincidence of both. This spirit—though by no means its dated forms—should be revived to create our own environment, with our new means of production, the machine.

But if they are not constantly checked and renewed, standards become stagnant. We know now that it is a futile attempt to try to match standards of the past, that our recent obsession with the idea that new buildings must always match existing ones betrayed a terrible weakness of our time, a silent admission of spiritual bankruptcy, for which there is no other example in the past. After the revolution in our own ranks, which has brought clarification, we seem to be set for a new creative effort. So it might be appropriate to investigate how far our professional framework fits the condition of our time, which I have tried to outline. Let's see whether the gigantic shift in the methods of production has been sufficiently recognised by us. For we have to see our case in the light of technological history and as we are not living in a period of sweet contemplation and security, we should reconsider our basic principles, for there are certainly some disturbing facts we cannot disregard any longer.

In the great periods of the past the architect was the 'master of the crafts' or 'master builder' who played a very prominent role within the whole production process of his time. But with the shift from crafts to industry he is no longer in this governing position.

Today the architect is not the 'master of the building industry.' Deserted by the best craftsmen (who have gone into industry, toolmaking, testing and researching), he has continued thinking in terms of the old craft methods, pathetically unaware of the colossal impact of industrialisation. The architect is in a very real danger of losing his grip in competition with the engineer, the scientist and the builder unless he adjusts his attitude and aims to meet the new situation.

SEPARATION OF DESIGN AND EXECUTION. Complete separation of design and execution of buildings, as it is in force today, seems to be altogether artificial if we compare it to the process of building in the great periods of the past. We have withdrawn much too far from that original and natural approach, when conception and realisation of a building were one indivisible process and when architect and builder were one and the same person. *The architect of the future—if he wants to rise to the top again—will be forced by the trend of events to draw closer once more to the building production.* If he will build up a closely co-operating team together with the engineer, the scientist and the builder, then design, construction and economy may again become an entity —a fusion of art, science and business.

I will be more specific and reveal my target: The American Institute of Architects at its 1949 convention added to the mandatory rules of the Institute a new paragraph which reads : 'An architect may not engage directly or indirectly in building contracting.'

I have very great doubts about the wisdom of this rule which would perpetuate the separation of design and construction. Instead we should try to find an organic reunification which would return to us the mastery of the know-how in building. Of course, the intention of this mandatory paragraph has been a good one, namely to block unfair competition. But I am afraid that it represents merely a negative veto and does not try to solve our dilemma constructively.

Let us not deceive ourselves as to the strength of our present position in the eyes of our clients. The average private client seems to consider us as members of a luxury profession whom he can call in if there is some extra money available for 'beautification.' He does not seem to consider us as essential for the building effort as the builder and the engineer.

If you think I exaggerate, look at the facts in the U.S.A. :

More than 80 per cent of all U.S. buildings are being built without an architect.

Average income of the architect is less than a bricklayer makes in the East.

People generally do not understand the complicated task of the architect as we define it, and we have not been able sufficiently to clarify the issue.

When a client is in the building mood, he wants to buy the complete building for a fixed price and at a definite time of delivery. He is not at all interested in the question of the division of labour between architect, engineer and contractor. Since he senses subconsciously that it is rather artificial to keep design and building so wide apart, he usually concludes that the architect may be the unknown 'X' in his calculations, in terms of money as well as time.

And what else can we expect? Are we not in an almost impossible position, having to meet a set price, though we have to start almost every commission with a kind of research and laboratory approach? Compare that with the long process in industry from paper design to test model to final product. In our field of design we have to absorb all the cost of research ourselves, for with us the model and the end product are one and the same. Has this not become an almost unsolvable task, particularly because it is subject to changes caused either by the client or by public agencies?

We often question the soundness of the business angle of our activities when we realise that the greater the ingenuity and the harder the work we devote to reducing costs, the more we are penalised by lesser payment. The client on the other hand assumes that it must be in the material interest of the architect to increase the building cost deliberately, since this would also increase the architect's percentage fee. So he often tries to settle for a lump sum fee. Of course we have to oppose that tendency of the client, as it is quite unfair to us, but that does not solve the ticklish problem in either direction. Here indeed is our greatest ethical dilemma. It often causes distrust on the part of the client, because of its inherent injustice to both parties; it even keeps many clients from seeking our service altogether.

EXAMPLE OF INDUSTRIAL DESIGNER. This does not happen to the designer of industrial products, who is usually paid for his initial service to develop the model, plus royalties from multiplication of the product. He benefits from the success of his work not only financially, but also in stature as a legitimate member of the team to which be belongs, along with the scientist, the engineer and the businessman. This process, developing more and more in industry, is carrying the previously isolated artist-designer back into the fold of society.

I am convinced that a similarly co-ordinated teamwork will also become the trend within the building industry. This should give the future architect, who is by vocation co-ordinator of the many activities concerned with building, once more the opportunity to become the master builder—if we are only willing to make the necessary changes in attitude and training. Of course, whether he shall be able, personally, to reach the high historical aim of his profession to integrate through his work all social, technical and aesthetic components into a comprehensive humanly appealing whole, that will depend on his creative vision. I say his 'aim' for whether he actually *is* the master depends of course on his performance within the collaborating team. He cannot claim leadership as such, for the best man in a team should lead. *But the historical mission of the architect has always been to achieve the complete co-ordination of all efforts in building up man's physical surroundings.* If he wants to be faithful to this high mission, he must train the rising generation in conformity with the new means of industrial production instead of confining them to a training at the platonic drafting board, isolated from making and building.

INDUSTRIALISATION AND PREFABRICATION. The machine certainly has not stopped at the threshold of building. The industrialisation process of building seems only to take longer to complete than it took in other fields of production, since building is so much more complex. One component part of building after another is being taken out of the hands of the craftsman and given to the machine. We have only to look at manufacturers' catalogues to become convinced that already an infinite variety of industrialised component building parts exists at our disposal. In a gradual evolutionary procedure, the hand-building process of old is being transformed into an assembly process of ready-made industrial parts sent from the factory to the site. Furthermore, the proportionate percentage of mechanical equipment in our buildings is steadily increasing. Prefabrication has penetrated much further into the building of skyscrapers than into residential building.

But, to be honest with ourselves, we must admit that only relatively few of us architects have directly taken part in influencing and performing this great change, or in designing those component parts which we all use in building. It is the engineer and the scientist who have been instrumental in this development. That is why we have to speed up to regain lost ground by training our young generation of architects for their twofold task : (1) to join the building industry and to take active part in developing and forming all those component parts for building, and (2) to learn how to compose beautiful buildings from these industrialised parts. This presupposes, in my opinion, much more direct participation and experience in the workshop and in the field in contact with industry and builders than our usual training provides.

The coming generation of architects must bridge that fatal gap between design and building.

To begin with, let's stop squabbling about styles ; every architect owes it to himself to defend the integrity of his design effort. What matters to the profession as a whole is to close ranks, to do some hard thinking together, and then to come to constructive decisions as to how we may reopen the gate leading into the field of building production for the benefit of the younger generation of architects. They are beginning to lose confidence in the trusteeship character of our professional set up and in its logical result : the self-appointed prima donna architect. *Architects in the future will refuse to be restrained from a natural urge to take actual part in a team effort with the industry to produce buildings and their parts. The emphasis, I believe, will be more and more on the team.*

TEAMWORK. For years I have been personally concerned through my activities as an educator, with the plight of young architects as they leave school and enter into practice. I have seen them make valiant attempts to establish themselves independently, and I have seen them more often resign themselves to work indefinitely as draughtsmen in large offices which offer little or no chance of exercising individual initative. It is sad to see so much youthful energy and talent dry up by the slow attrition of our more and more centralised working system. Democratic concepts cannot easily survive the assaults of our increasing mechanisation and super-organisation, unless an antidote is used which may protect the individual in his struggle against the levelling effect of the mass mind.

I have tried to find such an antidote by introducing my students in Harvard, besides their individual training, to the experience of working in teams. This has become a valuable stimulant to students as well as to teachers who were all equally unacquainted with the advantages and difficulties of collaborating in groups. Now they had to learn to collaborate without losing their identity. This is to me an urgent task lying before the new generation, not only in the field of architecture but in all our endeavours to create an integrated society.

In our particular field there is no book of rules for such collaboration, unless we go back as far as the Middle Ages to study the working teams of the great cathedral builders. Most striking within the organisation of those building guilds was the fact that until late in the eighteenth century every craftsman on the job was not an executing hand only, but was permitted to put his own design into his part of the work as long as he abided by the master's guiding key of design, which was the secret, geometrical auxiliary of the building guilds, similar to the keys in musical composition. Preconceived paper design hardly existed at all; the group lived together, discussed the task and built their ideas.

Compare this with our present conditions. We are expected to put all our design ideas, unto the last screw, into drawings and specifications. Then an army of workmen has to execute our design. We are hardly permitted to make any changes though there is no genius who could have sufficient foresight or imagination properly to judge the effect of every detail of his preconceived design; even less so the more he stays aloof from the practical process of building and making. Nor has the workman of today any chance to contribute to the design of a building. Since the time of the building guilds, collaboration among men, which would release the creative instincts of the individual instead of smothering them, has not been practised much and we find very little knowledge about the basic requirements which made such teamwork possible. It is so unknown today in our profession that it is apt to be even viewed with apprehension, because the ideology of the past century has taught us to see in the individual genius the only embodiment of true and pure art. *It is true that the creative spark originates always with the individual, but by working in close collaboration with others toward a common aim, he will attain greater heights of achievement through the stimulation and challenging critique of his teammates, than by living in an ivory tower.* Of course, the creative mind asserts itself usually under any circumstance, even against heavy odds, but if we want to raise the average performance, teamwork becomes essential to sharpen and improve the individual contribution.

The *conditio sine qua non* of true teamwork is voluntariness ; it cannot be established by command. It calls for an unprejudiced state of mind and for the firm belief that togetherness of thought and action is a prerequisite for the growth of human culture. Individual talent will assert itself quickly in such a group and will profit for its part from the crossfertilization of minds in the give and take of daily contact. True leadership can emerge when all members have a chance to become leaders by performance, not by appointment. Leadership does not depend on innate talent only, but very much on one's intensity of conviction and devotion to serve. Serving and leading seem to be interdependent.

Our time is probably as rich as any in original talent, but too often this is doomed to spend itself in isolated accidental bursts of creativity because its message is lost for lack of a comprehensive response. If we could reclaim the individual genius for his natural task, i.e., to work as a *primus inter pares*—first among equals—instead of in exalted isolation, a much broader basis for understanding and response could be formed.

Certainly good intention alone is not sufficient for building up a team. We have to relearn methods of collaboration. It takes considerable time to acquire certain habits which seem indispensable for fruiful teamwork. I discovered that it was first of all imperative that every participant of the team must tell the other members right from the start what he is thinking and doing in a continuous mutual exchange. But even if everyone has the best intention to proceed that way in the beginning, it takes quite a while to train oneself to this end. Then this exchange becomes indispensable, as it places the different individuals in the right place within the collaborating team and, of course, everyone likes to do what he is particularly fitted for. Research then grows quickly, and a variety of opinions develops into a challenge for the team to come to final terms. In the flood of so many objective problems that have to be solved, the natural vanity of the individual is slowly drowned. The task grows gradually above the individual, who finally hardly remembers who initiated this or that part of the idea, as all their thoughts resulted from mutual stimulation. The stature of the individual grows under this voluntary collective effort of the team. As democracy obviously hinges on our ability to co-operate, I want the architect, as a co-ordinator by vocation, to lead the way toward developing the new technique of collaboration in teams. The essence of such technique should be to emphasise individual freedom of initiative, instead of authoritative direction by a boss. Experimenting with teamwork keeps one resilient and flexible and its methods are probably more adaptable to the rapid changes of our time than the boss-employee relationship. *Synchronising all individual efforts the team can raise its integrated work to higher potentials than is represented by the sum of the work of just so many individuals.*

I should like to leave no doubt however that the type of

team which will be effective for future building must certainly reach into the field of production. Increasing specialisation needs ever growing co-ordination.

To accomplish the first of the twofold tasks of the future—the development of the component building parts—the architect needs to build up a team with the scientist and the manufacturer. His second task—the design of finished buildings from such component parts, and their actual assembly on the site—should be solved in a closely integrated collaboration between him, the engineer and the builder in direct contact with industrial methods and research.* It is quite obvious that we as individual architects have no facilities to test new materials and new technological methods, and even less to control our wealth of new technical potentialities the way the master builder of old controlled the crafts. In order to become more effective again for the whole process of building, we need the team and the production tools of industry. But we should not assume that our self-determined privilege to act as leader of the team will be accepted per se. As late-comers in industry we have to take the risk to join the team as equals and then to show by way of our own performance whether we shall be able to act as first among equals and so finally to change that rank order of public esteem in the architect's favour.

The essential difference of our industrialised society compared to a society of handcraftsmen rests upon the distribution of labour, not upon the tools used. A complicated textile machine represents only a refinement of the early hand loom. But it marks a change of principal importance if the entity of a working process is handled by one and the same craftsman, or if it is subdivided into many fragments, each of which is being put into the hands of another worker, as at the assembly line. It is this atomising effect of the subdivision of labour which has exploded the coherence of the premachine society,

---

* With this type of collaboration I do not refer to the so-called 'package deal' corporations, as they treat architectural design more or less as a minor appendix only to the all-important business transaction. In the team which I have in mind the designer must have as much power of decision as the businessman and the builder. He must be a legitimate partner.

not the machine itself. I confidently hope that organically built-up teamwork will gradually give us back that essential connectedness which is indispensable for a unity of effort.

I have merely tried to throw some light on the crossroad to which our profession has come. One of the two roads appears rough but wide and full of venture and hope. The other narrow one may lead into a dead end.

I have made my personal choice where to go, but being along in years, all I can do is to urge those who represent the next generation to search for a constructive solution how to correlate again design and execution in their future practice by direct participation in industrial and building production. For I cannot convince myself that it shows a lack of integrity when a young architect and a young builder decide to join hands in order to build up a complete modern service—both design and building execution. We should instead actively encourage such a natural combination.

I have been asked whether it would not leave the client high and dry when he is deprived of the trustee control of his architect. My reply is that we do not need trustees for buying our everyday goods ; we select them on account of the good reputation of the make or of the manufacturer. I do not see any difference as to buildings and their component parts. Of course, I know that the task of reconciling design and execution—which should be inseparable—will still meet a great many difficulties which can only be slowly solved in practice. But it is always a change of attitude first which precedes any implementation of a new course of direction.

This proposal I certainly do not think of as a cure-all for the ills that beset our profession. Nobody knows yet which measures will have to be taken to protect it against unfair competition, while at the same time giving the green light to those who want to take creative part also in the production itself of buildings and building parts. All I propose to do in today's state of fluidity is to keep the door open to a new set of problems, and knotty ones at that, which are the result of the impact of industrialisation and must be solved by the new generation of architects.

Architect—Servant or Leader?*

Modern architecture is not a few branches of an old tree—it is new growth coming right from the roots. This does not mean, however, that we are witness to the sudden advent of a 'new style.' What we see and experience is a movement in flux which has created a fundamentally different outlook on architecture. Its underlying philosophy knits well with the big trends in today's science and art, steadying it against those forces which try to block its advance and to retard the growing power of its ideas.

WHAT CONSTITUTES A 'STYLE'? The irrepressible urge of critics to classify contemporary movements which are still in flux by putting each neatly in a coffin with a style label on it has increased the widespread confusion in understanding the dynamic forces of the new movement in architecture and planning. What we looked for was a new approach not a new style. A style is a successive repetition of an expression which has become settled already as a common denominator for a whole period. *But the attempt to classify and thereby to freeze living art and architecture, while it is still in the formative stage, into a 'style' or 'ism' is more likely to stifle than to stimulate creative activity.* We live in a period of reshuffling our entire life; the old society went to pieces under the impact of the machine, the new one is still in the making. The flow of continuous growth, the change in expression in accordance with the changes of our life is what matters in our design work, not the hunt after formalistic 'style' features.

And how deceiving a precipitate terminology can be! Let us analyse, for instance, that most unfortunate designation,

* See: 'Eight Steps toward a Solid Architecture' by W. Gropius, *Architectural Forum*, New York, February, 1954.

'The International Style.' It is not a style because it is still in flux, nor is it international because its tendency is the opposite—namely, to find regional, indigenous expression derived from the environment, the climate, the landscape, the habits of the people.

Styles in my opinion should be named and outlined by the historian only for past periods. In the present we lack the dispassionate attitude necessary for impersonal judgment of what is going on. As humans we are vain and jealous and that distorts objective vision. Why don't we leave it, then, to the future historians to settle the history of today's growth in architecture and go to work and let it grow ? I'd like to suggest that in a period when the leading spirits of mankind try to see the human problems on earth as interdependent, as one world, any chauvinistic national prejudice regarding the shares claimed in the development of modern architecture must result in narrowing limitation. Why split hairs about who influenced whom when all that really matters is whether the results achieved improved our life ? I dare say that we are all much more influenced by each other today than architects of former centuries because of the rapid development of interchange and intercommunication. This should be welcome as it enriches us and promotes a common denominator of understanding so badly needed. (I tried to encourage my students to let themselves be influenced by ideas of others, as long as they feel able to absorb and digest them and to give them new life in a context that represents their own approach to design.)

SEARCH FOR COMMON DENOMINATOR VERSUS EGO CULT. If we look back to see what has been achieved during the last thirty or forty years we find that the artistic gentleman-architect who turned out charming Tudor mansions with all modern conveniences has almost vanished. This type of applied archeology is disappearing fast. *It is melting in the fire of our conviction that the architect should conceive buildings not as monuments but as receptacles for the flow of life which they have to serve, and that his conception must be flexible enough to create a background fit to absorb the dynamic features of our modern life.* We know that a period piece of architecture could never satisfy such a demand, but it is just as easy to create a modern straitjacket as a Tudor one—particularly if the architect approaches his task solely with the intention of creating a memorial to his own genius. This arrogant misapprehension of what a good architect should be often prevailed, even after the revolution against eclecticism had already set in. Designers who were searching for new expression in design would even outdo the eclecticist by striving to be 'different', to seek the unique, the unheard of, the stunt.

This cult of the ego has delayed the general acceptance of the sound trends in modern architecture. Remnants of this mentality must be eliminated before the true spirit of the architectural revolution can take root among the people everywhere and produce a common form expression of our time after almost half a century of trial and error. *This will presuppose a determined attitude of the new architect to direct his efforts toward finding the type, the best common denominator instead of toward the provocative stunt.* Preconceived ideas of form, whether the ·outcome of personal whims or fashionable styles, tend to force the stream of life in a building into rigid channels and to hamper the natural activities of the people therein.

The pioneers of the new movement in architecture developed methodically a new approach to the whole problem of 'design for living.' Interested in relating their work to the life of the people, they tried to see the individual unit as part of a greater whole. This social idea contrasts strongly with the work of the egocentric prima donna architect who forces his personal fancy on an intimidated client, creating solitary monuments of individual aesthetic significance.

THE CLIENT . By this statement I do not mean that we architects should docilely accept the client's views. We have to lead him into a conception which *we* must form to fit *his* needs. If he calls on us to fulfil some whims and fancies of his which do not make sense, we have to find out what real need may be behind these vague dreams of his and try to lead him in a consistent, over-all approach. We must spare no effort on our part to convince him conclusively and without conceit. We have to make the diagnosis of what the client needs on the strength of our competence. When a man is ill he certainly wouldn't insist on telling his physician how to treat him, but, if we expect such trust from our client, we learn that architects are rarely treated with the respect accorded to the medical profession. If we have not been competent enough to deserve being trusted, we had better make sure that we are in the future—in design, in construction and in economy, as well as in the social conception, which embraces the three other components of our work. If we neglect to make ourselves highly competent in all these fields, or if we shun responsibility in leading the way, we resign ourselves to the level of minor technicians.

Architecture needs conviction and leadership. It cannot be decided upon by clients or by Gallup Polls, which would most often only reveal a wish to continue what everybody knows best.

MACHINE AND SCIENCE IN SERVICE OF HUMAN LIFE. There is another argument going on which, distorting the aims of modern architecture, needs clarification. We hear : 'The modern accent is on living, not on the machine,' and 'Le Corbusier's slogan, The house is a machine for living,' is old hat. With it goes a portrait of the early pioneers of the modern movement as men of rigid, mechanistic conceptions, addicted to the glorification of the machine and quite indifferent to intimate human values. Being one of these monsters myself, I wonder how we managed to survive on such meagre fare. The truth is that the problem of how to humanise the machine was in the foreground of our early discussions and that a new way of living was the focus of our thoughts.

To devise new means to serve human ends, the Bauhaus, for instance, made an intense attempt to live what it preached and to find the balance in the struggle for utilitarian, aesthetic and psychological demands. *Functionalism was not considered a rationalistic process merely. It embraced the psychological*

G

problems as well. The idea was that our design should function both physically and psychologically. We realised that emotional needs are just as imperative as any utilitarian ones and demand to be satisfied. The machine and the new potentialities of science were of greatest interest to us, but the emphasis was not so much on the machine itself as on better use of the machine and science in the service of human life. Looking back, I find that our period has dealt too little with the machine, not too much.

WHAT IS REGIONAL EXPRESSION? Another confusing factor in the development of modern architecture is the appearance now and then of deserters from our cause who fall back on nineteenth-century eclecticism for lack of strength to go consistently through with a rejuvenation from the roots up. Designers turn back to features and fancies of the past to be mixed into the modern design, fondly believing that this will create greater popularity for modern architecture. They are too impatient to reach their goal by legitimate means and so they only conjure up a new 'ism' instead of a new genuine regional expression. True regional character cannot be found through sentimental or imitative approach by incorporating either old emblems or the newest local fashions which disappear as fast as they appear. But if you take, for instance, the basic difference imposed on architectural design by the climatic conditions of California, say, as against Massachusetts, you will realise what diversity of expression can result from this fact alone if the architect will use the utterly contrasting indoor-outdoor relations of these two regions as focus for his design conception.

Here I should like to mention one problem that all architectural schools have in common : as long as our teaching centres only around the platonic drafting board we are perpetually in danger of raising the 'precocious designer.' For it is almost unavoidable that the lack of practical experience in the field, in the crafts and industrial processess of building leads at least some students to an all too ready acceptance of current style ideas, fads and clichés. This is the consequence of an all too academic training. Therefore, any opportunity to go into the field and to take part in all or any phases of the building process should be readily grasped by the young designer as a most essential discipline to establish balance between knowledge and experience.

SERVICE AND LEADERSHIP. But you might say, 'What has this to do with the topic of this article: Architect—Servant or Leader ?' The answer, already implicit in what I have said before, is simple : put an 'and' in place of the 'or.' Serving and leading seem to be interdependent. The good architect must serve the people and simultaneously show real leadership built up upon a real conviction : leadership to guide his client as well as the working team entrusted with the job. Leadership does not depend on innate talent only, but very much also on one's intensity of conviction and willingness to serve. How can he reach this status ? I have often been asked by students what I could advise them to do to become independent architects after leaving school and how they could avoid selling out their conviction to a society still pretty ignorant of the new ideas in architecture and planning.

My answer is this :

Making a living cannot be the only aim of a young man who should want above all to realise his own creative ideas. Your problem is, therefore, how to keep the integrity of your conviction intact, how to live what you preach, and still find your pay. You may not succeed in finding a position with an architect who shares your approach in design and who could give you further guidance. Then I would suggest you take a paying job wherever you can sell your skill, but keep your interests alive by a consistent effort carried on in leisure hours. Try to build up a working team with one or two friends in your neighbourhood, choose a vital topic within your community, and try to solve it, step by step, in group work. Put ceaseless effort into it, then someday you will be able to offer the public, together with your group, a well-substantiated solution for this problem, for which you have become an expert. Meanwhile, publish it, exhibit it and you may succeed in becoming an adviser to your community authorities. Create strategic centres where people are confronted with a new reality and then try to weather the inevitable stage of violent criticism until people have learned to redevelop their atrophied physical and mental capacities to make the proper use of the proffered new set-up. We have to discern between the vital, real needs of the people and the pattern of inertia and habit that is so often advanced as 'the will of the people.'

The stark and frightening realities of our world will not be softened by dressing them up with the 'new look' and it will be equally futile to try to humanise our mechanised civilisation by adding sentimental fripperies to our homes. *But if the human factor is becoming more and more dominant in our work, architecture will reveal the emotional qualities of the designer in the very bones of the buildings, not in the trimmings only ; it will be the result of both good service and good leadership.*

III

Planning and Housing

The sections under this chapter are mostly contributions I made to the CIAM—Congrés Internationaux d'Architecture Moderne—which is the most vital and consistent international organisation aiming at 'Total Architecture.' The following statement was written for its twenty-fifth anniversary :

CIAM 1928—1953*

During the twenty-five years of its existence I have been a devoted member of the CIAM. Now it seems fitting that I express myself as to what this international stronghold of architects and planners has meant to me during the long fight for a new architecture.

The most important was the fact that in a world full of confusion, of piecemeal efforts, a small, supranational group of architects felt the necessity to rally in an effort to see the many-sided problems that confronted them as a totality.

The decision to put this conception of totality above all limited objectives has determined our attitude, our convictions, our faith. It is this idea that acted like a magnetic force under the most diverse conditions and among groups of widely different national and racial traditions. It started in Europe, but today it reaches to the four corners of the earth. That has enriched us. The fact that the racial or national genius of different countries often tends to be preoccupied with one particular approach to our common adventure in living to the exclusion of others makes us feel how badly we need the corrective stimulus of other forms of living, emphasising different values.

For instance : it seems that the youngest generation in the U.S.A.—down to the five-year-olds—is wholly fascinated by the problems of the conquest of outer space. They watch breathlessly as the scientists of the world are beginning to chart our way to the stars—even before we have succeeded in settling our earthly affairs. Their imagination is looking for new frontiers, almost unmindful of the confusion and derange-

---

* The CIAM—Congrés Internationaux d'Architecture Moderne—was established in 1928 in Château La Sarraz, Switzerland. The author has been one of its vice-presidents since 1929. For the aims and statutes of the CIAM see : *Can Our Cities Survive?* by J. L. Sert, Oxford University Press.

ment created during this ardent dash toward the unknown.

Brought face to face with the problems and blessings of those parts of the world that we call 'the underdeveloped countries,' we find their cultures have often given us a clearer insight into the deepest motives of human living than the complicated civilisations that we have created for ourselves. At this point we sometimes seem to regret the loss of their ancient roots and ties even more than they do themselves, but it would be a great mistake to think that they could preserve their integrity if they did not take part in the evolutionary process that binds us together now. The one thing they usually remember more distinctly than any of us is the fact that man lives also for the pursuit of happiness and I wish there would be more research by architects into what exactly are the prerequisites for this thing called 'happiness.' There was a time when architects were tempted to think that the possession of a non-leaking roof was the most important requirement for happiness, but we have since found out that though it may stop the rain, it does not necessarily create a happy human climate.

I want to affirm, therefore, that *I believe the creation of beauty and the forming of values and standards to be the innermost desire of a human being and that this moves him more deeply and more lastingly than the satisfactions of comfort. In our daily struggle to put that non-leaking roof over the heads of unsheltered millions we forget this too easily.*

CIAM, I confidently hope, will go on fighting for its original conception of totality with man as the measure for all our problems in planning and architecture.

Sociological Premises for the Minimum Dwelling of Urban Industrial Populations*

The over-all progress in housing design during the years following the First World War reveals that development of the minimum dwellings has reached a stalemate, evidently because deep-rooted changes in the social structure of nations which require the establishment of new standards in regard to the type and size of the necessary dwelling units have not received adequate attention. Determination of these changes in society must be the starting point for any work in this direction. Recognition of the evolutionary development of man's biological and sociological life processes must lead to a definition of the task at hand ; only after this has been accomplished will it be possible to solve the second part of the problem, the establishment of a practical programme for realising the minimum dwelling.

The history of sociology is the story of man's gradual evolution from the wilderness through barbarism to civilisation. The late German sociologist Müller-Lyer,† whose scientific results are referred to, distinguishes between four major legal eras of human society :

1. The era of kinship and tribal law.
2. The era of the family and family law.
3. The era of the individual and individual law.
4. The future era of co-operatives and communal law.

He establishes these as the successive phases of gradual social refinement. A detailed examination of these phases is useful because their regularity shows clearly that certain phenomena

* See : 'Die soziologischen Grundlagen der Minimalwohnung,' *Die Justiz,* Vol. 5, No. 8, (1929), Verlag Dr. Walther Rothschild, Berlin-Grunewald.

† Dr. F. Müller-Lyer, *Die Entwicklungsstufen der Menschheit* [*Man's Phases of Development*], J. F. Lehman, Munich, 1912.

in modern society which are regarded by many as manifestations of regressive decay are actually evidence of evolutionary progress in a society which is in the process of stratification.

In prehistoric times the individual is only a member of society ; his actions are purely social. The individual is not yet awakened.

The first signs of beginning individualism manifest themselves in the subjugation of woman by man. The patriarchal family arises and persists up to the formation of our modern industrial state.

The subjugation of woman is followed by the enslavement of man by the ruler. Stratification of society into lords and serfs liberates the ruling class so that it can devote itself to higher cultural problems. The masses are trained to labour, but the rights of the individual are suppressed.

Rule by force in the warring state is followed by rule by money in the industrial state. In both states the propertied class rules, the masses become inpoverished. The industrial state, inspired by increasing scientific knowledge, develops more advanced methods of production. The exploitation of nature offers the possibility of a life worthy of culture for all. Egotistical individualism gives way to social individualism. The fully developed individual becomes the aim of the state and the structure of society the means for its achievement.

Thus the concept of the tribe and the patriarchal family evolves into the ideal of an independent individual and finally into that of a future communal union which transcends the individual.

Inspired by the economic life of nations, the idea of rationalisation is today growing into a major intellectual movement in which the actions of the individual are gradually being brought into beneficial relation with the welfare of society as· a whole, a concept which transcends that of economic expediency for the individual alone. From the motive of 'reason', social consciousness arises.

This evolutionary process is paralleled by changes in the structure and significance of the family.

The patriarchal family was characterised by supreme sovereignty of the family head. The wife lived in intellectual sterility and subjugation, and the children, even when grown up, were subordinated by absolute obedience to the will of the family head. Relatives and serfs, later the servants, apprentices and journeymen, were members of the larger family. The family was a self-sufficient microcosm, the unit of production and consumption in the state.

The eighteenth century marks the flight of serfs from the feudal master household to the free cities. The number of small families with their structure of parental sovereignty increases.

With the spread of the concept of the rights of the individual, the family progressively surrenders its functions to the state and thus the importance of the family unit in the sociological picture gradually decreases.

The invention of the machine leads to the socialisation of labour. Goods are no longer produced for one's own needs but for the purpose of exchange within the society. One product of domestic industry after another is wrested from the family and transferred to socialised industry. The smaller unit, the family, thus loses its character as a self-contained productive unit.

With the progressive emergence of the individual the human birth rate decreases, in a manner analogous to phenomena observed in other forms of life, and it decreases in all civilised countries. The will of the individual, armed with the means provided by scientific achievements, tends toward voluntary birth control for reasons of predominantly economic nature. Within the span of one single generation the two-child pattern is established in all the civilised countries.

On the basis of surveys in the European countries and in America, the average family may be assumed to comprise 4.5 members. This number is averaged over urban as well as rural districts. The average family size in larger cities is below 4 throughout.

According to determinations by the German census bureau (1928), the birth rate in Germany was 35.6 per 1,000 population in the year 1900, and 18.4 per 1,000 population in the year 1927. It had thus decreased to a mere half. Nonetheless, there is still a birth excess of 6.4 per thousand.

In other civilised countries the decline in birth rate and the resulting decrease in family size progresses at a similar pace. The birth rate in the various countries decreases with increasing industrialisation, but there is still an excess of births in them all.

In the patriarchal system the family alone was responsible for raising its children. Nowadays the state places a portion of the children's education in the hands of specially trained pedagogues in public schools. It thus intrudes into the relations between parents and children and regulates them according to the views of society. It establishes social security laws to provide insurance for old age, disease and physical handicap and thereby gradually relieves the family of its responsibility to care for the aged, the sick and the handicapped.

Whereas the sons in a patriarchal family inherited their father's trade, this caste system is dying out and the vocational castes which supersede the birth castes promote early departure from the parental home. The individual's mobility increases with the increasing transportation facilities, and the family is thereby diffused and diminished.

The patriarchal relationship between the family head and the journeymen, servants and apprentices is replaced by financial relationships as the barter economy is displaced by the financial economy. The activities of the family have become too limited to occupy all its members. The family domicile has become too expensive and too confined to shelter and employ the grown-up children permanently.

The former serfs become free servants, but with the progressive socialisation of labour their number gradually decreases as more and more of them escape the family yoke to seek personal freedom and independence in industry. In most European countries today the demand for domestic servants exceeds the supply by a factor of two. In the United States the shortage of domestic help is already causing families to move into hotels, in which the domestic chores of the small family are economically centralised.

The confined dwelling is also losing its suitability for social intercourse, and intellectual inspiration is sought outside the family circle ; the number of restaurants and clubs for men and women is increasing rapidly.

The rented apartment is replacing the ancestral family home, attachment to the home town ceases, and a new era of nomad individuals begins, fostered by the rapid development of mechanised transportation. The family is losing its home just as the tribe lost its territory. The cohesive power of the family is yielding to the rights of the individual citizen of the state. The conditions of socialised production enable the independent individual to change his place of employment at will, and population mobility is increasing tremendously. Most of the former family functions are gradually being assumed by society, and the importance of the family decreases despite its continued existence, while the state as such becomes institutionalised.

Past development thus shows steadily progressing socialisation of former family functions of legal, pedagogic and domestic nature, and thus we perceive the first beginnings of a communal era which might someday displace the era of individual rights.

One further phenomenon has a decisive effect on the structure of the modern family. As the family era was ushered in by the rise of man, so the individual era is characterised by the awakening and progressive emancipation of woman. Woman's duty of obedience to man vanishes, and the laws of society gradually grant her rights equal to those of men. As the family transfers numerous domestic chores to the machinery of socialised production, woman's sphere of domestic activity shrinks and she looks beyond the family for an outlet for her natural need for occupation : she enters the world of business and industry. In turn industry, rejuvenated on basically new foundations by the machine, shows woman the impractical nature of her domestic hand labour.

Recognition of the shortcomings of the individual household awakens thoughts about new forms of centralised master households which partially relieve the individual woman of her domestic tasks by means of an improved centralised organisation which is capable of performing them better and more economically than she can perform them herself, even when she applies all her efforts. The growing shortage of domestic help further emphasises such desires. In the hard battle for subsistence faced by the entire family, the woman seeks ways of gaining free time for herself and her children while participating in gainful occupations and liberating herself from dependence upon the man. Thus the process does not seem to be motivated exclusively by the economic plight of urban populations, but it is the manifestation of an internal drive which is connected with the intellectual and economic emancipation of woman to equal partnership with man.

The organisational structure of such master households for single men and women, for children, widowed or divorced adults, for newlyweds or for ideological and economic communities of various forms is connected intimately with the problem of the minimum dwelling.

It is of course true that even in the present age, for which our practical work is intended, all forms of human society, old and new, continue to exist side by side ; it is quite obvious, however, that one form predominates at any given time ; the importance of the individual and his independent rights today overshadows that of the family as a sovereign unit. The rise to independence of the woman dissolved a powerful family bond ; the forced marriage of old has practically vanished, and France in the days of the Revolution already considered marriage legally as merely a contract between citizens, which implies the right to divorce ; woman finally achieved suffrage and thus political equality with man. Liberated from the limited horizon of the household, she extends her influence to cultural spheres.

The increasing independence achieved by woman produces modifications of a fundamental nature in the cornerstone of the family, the marriage contract. Originally, a compulsory institution sanctioned by the state and the church, it evolves gradually into a voluntary union of persons who retain their intellectual and economic independence. Economically speaking, the family is reduced to the functions of reproduction and breeding selection. The stronger the organisation of the social contract, the smaller the sphere remaining to the family. In its trend toward collective thinking, the institution of individualism is following the path pursued by its forerunner, the institution of family supremacy.

The evolutionary development outlined above is reflected by the following statistics, furnished by the German census bureau :

Divorces	1900	9,000
	1927	36,449
Illegitimate births	1900	8.7%
	1926	12.6%

In addition, according to information from physicians which it is difficult to obtain statistically, the number of abortions has increased substantially :

Individual households	
1871	6.16%
1910	7.26%
1927	10.1%

The ratio of the number of gainfully employed women to that of gainfully employed men (1920-21) :

United States	1 : 4
Belgium	1 : 3
England and Sweden	2 : 5
Germany and Switzerland	1 : 2

According to information supplied by the Prussian district census bureau for Berlin in 1925 :

Of 5 women above 20, only 3 are married.

Of 3 gainfully employed persons, 2 are men and 1 is a woman.

Of 5 married women, 1 is gainfully employed.

Of 5 single women, 4 are gainfully employed.

Of 2 gainfully employed women, 1 is simultaneously a housewife.

In 1927 46% of all dwellings in Germany have only 1—3 rooms.

Policy-making government agencies charged with housing administration find it necessary, first of all, to observe the trends of social development, because the most difficult phase of their activity is the correct numerical estimation of the extent to which these general developments will progress within the population of their jurisdictional area. Only after formulation of this estimate are they in a position to distinguish between the numerical requirements for resolving both the older, familiar types of housing shortages, wherever they are still pronounced, as well as the newer, more individually differentiated needs, and to assign suitable housing to both groups. Almost all districts are still basing their policies of urban housing procurement to an excessive extent upon the old familial form of life, a pattern which by itself is no longer capable of describing the actual problems. It appears, instead, that the combination of a number of apartments in the form of a centralised master household has become necessary in order to lighten the burden of gainfully employed women and thus preserve them for marriage and reproduction.

The sociological facts must first be clarified in order that the ideal minimum of a life necessity, the dwelling, and the minimum cost of its production may be found ; in view of the change in underlying principles, the programme for a minimum dwelling can naturally not be solved by simply reducing the conventional, larger apartment in number of rooms and effective area. An entirely new formulation is required, based on a knowledge of the natural and sociological minimum requirements, unobscured by the veil of traditionally imagined historical needs. We must attempt to establish facts and geographic and climatic conditions. This approach is in the spirit of the impending equalisation of life requirements under the influence of travel and world trade.

The problem of the minimum dwelling is that of establishing the elementary minimum of space, air, light and heat required by man in order that he be able to fully develop his life functions without experiencing restrictions due to his dwelling, i.e., a minimum *modus vivendi* in place of a *modus non moriendi*.

The actual minimum varies according to local conditions of city and country, landscape and climate ; a given quantity of air space in the dwelling has different meanings in a narrow city street and in a sparsely settled suburb. Von Drigalski, Paul Vogler and other hygienists observe that, given good conditions of ventilation and sunlight, man's requirements of living space from the biological viewpoint are very small, particularly if the space is correctly organised for efficiency ; a graphic picture of the superiority of a small modern apartment over an obsolete one is provided by the comparison offered by a well-known architect between an ingeniously arranged ward-robe trunk and a crate.

However, if the provision of light, sun, air and warmth is culturally more important and, with normal land prices, more economical than an increase in space, then the rules dictate : enlarge the windows, reduce the size of rooms, economise on food rather than heat. Just as it was formerly customary to over-estimate the value of food calories in comparison with that of vitamins, many people nowadays erroneously regard larger rooms and larger apartments as the desirable aim in dwelling design.

To allow for the increasing development of more pro-nounced individuality of life within the society and the indi-vidual's justified demand for occasional withdrawal from his surroundings, it is necessary, moreover, to establish the fol-lowing ideal minimum requirement : *every adult shall have his own room, small though it may be!* The basic dwelling implied by these fundamental requirements would then repre-sent the practical minimum which fulfills its purpose and intentions : the standard dwelling.

The same biological considerations which determine the size of the minimum dwelling are also determinative in regard to its grouping and incorporation into the city plan. *Maximum light, sun and air for all dwellings!* In view of differences in the quality of the air and the intensity of the light, an attempt must be made to establish a numerically defined lower limit, on the basis of which the required amount of light and air can be calculated for given local conditions. General quantita-tive regulations which fail to allow for differences, as they

H

exist at present, are useless in many cases. To be sure, it is the basic aim of all urban building codes to ensure light and air for dwellings. Every new building code has surpassed its predecessor in striving to decrease the population density and thereby to improve conditions of light and air. However, all means employed thus far for decreasing population density are based on the concept of the permanent, close-knit family. The only ideal solution was thought to be the single detached dwelling, the one-family house with garden, and on the basis of this aim the excessive population density of cities was combatted by limiting building height. However, this aim is no longer adequate today, as sociology shows, because it satisfies only a portion of the public needs, but not the needs of the industrial population, which is the primary object of our investigations. The internal structure of the industrial family makes it turn from the one-family house toward the multistorey apartment house, and finally toward the centralised master household. The healthy tendency to progressively decrease the population density in cities is in no way endangered by this new form of dwelling, since the population density of a zone can be controlled without limiting the building height by merely establishing a quantitative ratio of dwelling area or building volume to building lot area. This would pave the way for a vertical development of the multi-storey apartment building. Whereas the detached one-family house is more suited to the needs of other, wealthier population classes which are not under consideration at present, the large apartment building satisfies more nearly the sociological requirements of present-day industrial populations with their symptomatic liberation of the individual and early separation of the children from the family. In addition, the large high-rise apartment building offers considerable cultural advantages as compared to the walk-up department house with a small number of floors. For a comparison in the case of alternating parallel blocks of apartments with north-south orientation and having blocks of varying height (two to ten floors), see Fig. 40, a, b, c, d.

The results derived from this comparison ensure that the large high-rise apartment building will have the biologically important advantages of more sun and light, larger distances between neighbouring buildings, and the possibility of providing extensive, connected parks and play areas between the blocks. It thus appears necessary to develop the well-organised high-rise apartment building technically, incorporating in its design the ideas of the centralised master household, i.e., to develop gradually the centralisation and specialisation of the domestic work associated with the small family. Such a large apartment house does not represent a necessary evil accompanying a period of regressive decay, but a biologically motivated, genuine residential building type of the future for urban industrial populations.

The objections of one-sided defenders of houses against the idea of the residential skyscraper on the grounds that natural instincts attach man to the ground are without biological foundation.

Modern urban industrial population is derived directly from the rural population. It retains its primitive standard of living, which frequently even decreases, instead of developing expanded requirements corresponding to its new way of life. The attempt to adapt its housing requirements to its old form of life appears regressive for the reasons described and altogether incompatible with its new form of life.

Previous experience in the various countries reveals that there is a gap between the cost of producing dwellings and the average income of the families. It is thus not possible to satisfy the housing requirements of the masses within the framework of a free economy. As a result, the state is beginning to relieve the family provider of a portion of his responsibilities in this respect as well and to gradually equalise the discrepancies caused by present rent levels with the aid of subsidies and other measures. Indeed, the construction of low-cost dwellings offers little temptation to industry and banking, whose natural tendency it is to derive maximum profits from production and investments. Since technology operates within the framework of industry and finance and since any cost reduction achieved must first of all be exploited for the benefit of private industry, it will only be able to provide cheaper and more varied dwellings if the government increases private industry's interest in dwelling construction by increased wel-fare measures. If the minimum dwelling is to be realised at rent levels which the population can afford, the government must therefore be requested to :

1. Prevent the waste of public funds for apartments of excessive size, while facilitating the financing of the construc-tion of minimum dwellings, for which an upper limit of apart-ment size must be established.

2. Reduce the initial cost of roads and utilities.

3. Provide the building sites and remove them from the hands of speculators.

4. Liberalise as far as possible the zoning regulations and building codes.

On the average, one-quarter of the income is considered a tolerable rent. It will have to be determined whether or not the programme to be planned can be realised within the scope of actual rent levels.

However, present-day minimum requirements of apartment hunters, which are a result of impoverishment, should not serve as a criterion for establishing the minimum dwelling if an absolute, biologically motivated result is to be achieved ; it would therefore also be incorrect to base the programme on the present income of the average family. Instead, the prop-erly established standard, the 'rationed dwelling,' must become the minimum requirement of every gainfully employed person ; it then is up to the community to find means for making this 'rationed dwelling' accessible to all the employed.

Houses, Walk-ups or High-rise Apartment Blocks?*

What is the most rational building height in the grouping of low-cost dwellings from the viewpoint of city planning? To clarify the problem, it seems expedient to first define more closely the concept 'rational.' The term literally means 'according to reason,' and thus in the present case it implies not only economic considerations, but primarily also those of psychological and sociological nature. The sociological aspects of a wholesome housing policy are unquestionably of more vital importance than the purely economic aspects, because economics for all its importance is not an end in itself but only a means to an end. Rationalisation therefore makes sense only if it tends to enrich life or, in the language of economics, if it spares the most precious of commodities, the vitality of the people.

Currently valid opinions concerning building heights to be considered expedient in urban dwelling construction are characterised by the following sentences from the German *Government Directives for the Housing Industry* for the year 1929 :

' The dwellings must be provided in buildings which satisfy modern health requirements, particularly in regard to adequate illumination and ventilation. These requirements are best satisfied by small house construction in the wider sense of the word. The aim should be one-family dwellings with gardens. If local conditions require large apartment houses, the height of such buildings is to be limited to a

* See : CIAM, *Rationelle Bebauungsweisen*, 'Flach—Mittel—oder Hochbau ?' by Walter Gropius, pp. 26—47, Verlag Englert & Schlosser, 1931. 'Das Wohnhochhaus' by W. Gropius, *Das Neue Frankfurt*, February 1931, Internationale Monatsschrift, Frankfurt/M.

maximum of three residential stories in medium-size towns and to a maximum of four residential stories in larger cities Only in special cases in several metropolitan cities should these heights be exceeded, and even in these cases a decrease in building heights by zoning laws should be strived for, particularly in outlying districts.'

The attitude reflected by these words, which is probably paralleled to a somewhat less pronounced extent in the majority of other countries, was initially inspired by the sound intention to reduce the population density in cities which in many cases has become excessive, mainly due to real estate speculation. It is up to the government to act in the general interest in remedying the tragic situation in which the very land we live on is subjected to the market manipulations of the business world.

The ravages following wild building activity in the cities brought about the healthy reaction of a back-to-nature trend and a battle of authorities and private citizens to settle the majority of the population in one-family houses with gardens. This form of dwelling is undoubtedly excellent in many respects, and public measures to promote single dwelling construction are to be welcomed. It is a fallacy, on the other hand, to apply the natural tendency toward height limitation in house construction to the multi-family dwelling as well, because the aim of reducing population density can be achieved by more rational procedures than the usual 'down-zoning.' Suggestions in regard to this important problem will follow later. Economic experience gained during the past years and readjustments in the living and dwelling habits of many social classes leave no doubt that the one-sided efforts in favour of individual home production resulted in a neglect of apartment house construction and led to confusion which had a detrimental effect on the entire housing policy. According to the present state of affairs, the tendency to house the majority of the population in detached dwellings is undoubtedly an economic utopia. But is this aim at all justified? Is the one-family house with a garden borrowed from country life in every respect the ideal solution for the urban industrial popu-

lation which longs for nature? Does this type of housing in
itself ensure the full physical and spiritual development of its
occupants? Is a reasonable development of the city conceivable
if all its citizens live in single homes with gardens? I do not
think so. But let us examine the basic premises of the problem
in order that we may define the optimum limits between
houses and high-rise apartment blocks.

P R E M I S E S . Violently conflicting opinions concerning the
ideal type of housing persist : the root of the controversy is
the old antithesis of city versus country. Man requires contrasts for stimulation and relaxation, and the urbanite's long-
ing for the country as well as the country dweller's long-
ing for the city are elementary drives constantly in need of
satisfaction. Progressing development ameliorates the sharp
contrast by bringing the comforts of the city to the country
and returning the charms of nature to the city. The less this
double drive is satisfied (and this frustration is more or less
prevalent, particularly in large cities), the more violent the
battle for equalising factors, such as the house in a garden. The
battle for the ideal type of housing is psychological in its
origin and consequently subject to panicky reversals and
psychoses such as the one we observed in the passionate fight
against the tenements.

*The essentials for wholesome life are, in addition to adequate
food and warmth : light, air and elbow room.* Undoubtedly
these three cardinal conditions for a livable dwelling are more
completely satisfied by the one-family house than by the
tabooed cold water flats in crowded tenement sections. However, the cause for the misery of these undignified dwellings
is not the dwelling form of the multi-storey apartment house
as such but the shortsighted legislation which permitted the
construction of this class of low-cost dwellings to fall into
the hands of unscrupulous speculators without adequate
social safeguards. Responsibly planned high-rise apartment
blocks situated on wide expanses of green with ample space
between them are certainly capable of satisfying all the requirements of light, air and elbow room while simultaneously
offering the urbanite a wealth of other advantages.

The special character of metropolitan housing developments for settling large numbers of working people around a concentrated city core makes for short travelling distances, which implies the use of multi-storey construction to reduce horizontal distances. The single-family house is contradictory to this basic trend of the city. It is the task of the city planner not merely to improve transportation facilities, but rather to reduce the need for them. The citizens of Los Angeles, by area the largest city of the world and consisting almost exclusively of single homes, spend a large fraction of each day travelling to and from their places of work or business ; their sacrifice of time and money for daily travel is many times that of the German working population, whose average travelling distance is long enough as it is. The director of the research institute for hygiene and immunisation of the Kaiser-Wilhelm Institute in Berlin, Dahlem, Professor Friedberger, calculates the average travelling expenses of a gainfully employed family of four in Berlin which is forced to live in the suburbs while working in the city to be 139 per cent of a typical peacetime rent ; in twenty-five years and assuming an interest rate of only 3.5 per cent, this travelling cost adds up to an amount equal to twice the cost of building an inexpensive dwelling. Assuming a travelling trip of only half an hour to and from work, he finds that the 2,200,000 working people in Berlin spend a total of 37,500,000 eight-hour working days each year travelling; each individual loses two working years during an average working life of thirty years. Imagine what the corresponding figures for Los Angeles would be !

Thus for the average low-income population, suburban life is uneconomical. To quote Friedberger's conclusion from his investigations :

' High-rise buildings surrounded by as much landscaping as possible thus appear to be the only housing type suitable for metropolitan areas. The sins of a fallacious housing policy and particularly of incorrect land use during the growth period of our metropolitan cities have virtually brought the only type of housing appropriate for large cities into disrepute. The natural reaction to the justly despised, improperly executed and exploited 'tenement' inspired a general desire for individual homes, the migration toward the suburbs of metropolitan cities. The movement was not based as much on rational considerations as on wishful thinking tinged by emotional bias. Unfortunately the iron laws of economics do not yield to wishful housing policies. Public welfare standards which are too highly aimed are actually injurious to the public insofar as they make it impossible to provide that which is actually economically feasible for the largest possible number of people.

Sober economic considerations are too easily overshadowed by the dream of a single home.'

Friedberger's verdict carries all the more weight, coming from a responsible hygienist.

The opponents of urban apartment houses ascribe decreases in the birth rate and the spread of diseases to the crowded living conditions in large cities, an accusation which certainly seems plausible on the surface. But strangely enough, certain important facts contradict this assumption. Although according to the volume for 1928 of the *Statistical Report on Germany*, the over-all birth rate for the entire country is 18.6 per thousand population, while the figure for all large cities is only 13.6, the rate averaged over the Western industrial regions of particularly high population density is 20 per thousand and thus exceeds the over-all average for the entire country. Von Drigalski, city health official in Berlin, and Krautwig, hygienist in Cologne, observe that the spread of communicable diseases is in no way connected with crowded living conditions and the small size of dwellings, but with the inadequate illumination and ventilation of substandard apartments which, in addition, are occupied by undernourished low-income groups.

In his 'Investigation Concerning Living Conditions, Particularly in Small Apartments,' Friedberger debunks the dogma that the worst living conditions are found in large cities. Simultaneously, on the basis of research by others (Karl Flügge) as well as his own careful investigation of urban and rural living conditions he arrives at the conclusion that theories concerning impairment of health due to living conditions, particularly in large cities, have suffered severely.

If we can rely on these pronouncements it follows that *apartment houses are above reproach from the health viewpoint, providing of course that good conditions of illumination and ventilation are provided. The two extreme types of housing, low and high, are thus not inherently good or bad, but their different characteristics require different applications.* Let us compare :

The occupant of an individual home buys the advantages of more quiet and outdoor life in sparsely settled residential districts in exchange for the disadvantages of long travelling distances, loss of spare time in crowded public conveyances with danger of infection, long distances to school for the children and more difficult shopping. The occupant of an apartment house, on the other hand, must pay for the time gained due to decreased horizontal distances with the loss of direct access to the outdoors and the necessity of using stairs or elevators. The single home with a garden is more suitable for families with children in higher-income brackets who are permanently settled and do not depend on changes in place of employment and on repeated moving, while the rented dwelling in an apartment house is better adapted to the needs of the more mobile working class. The one-family house fails to meet the needs, in regard to cost or otherwise, of this largest group of housing consumers because its universal introduction is prohibited, not by the ravages of a capitalistic society, but by the very nature of cities. Dr. Martin Wagner, former building commissioner of Berlin, a passionate defender of house construction, considers it an established fact that the one-family house is not feasible as a minimum dwelling but only for larger families, and that, moreover, its initial cost and site requirements are greater than in the case of an apartment home of equal size. These facts are inescapable, and therefore the one-family house will remain reserved for a higher stratum of the population. However, since it undoubtedly offers many valuable contributions to family life, particularly with a view to children, the government must promote the distribution and construction of this type of housing wherever the need for single homes exists, even if the economic difficulties involved are greater than in the case of apartment house construction. In choosing a type of housing one should not only compare the cost of construction, but also the cost of maintenance in time and money. The latter item in particular is larger in the case of the one-family house, especially if travelling costs are included. In particular, also, low-income families lack the time required to care for a house and garden if they are not to deteriorate.

There is an undeniable need to liberate the overworked housewife in the average urban low-income family by labour-saving devices in the home so that she will have free time for herself and her children and be able to contribute to the family income. It should also be borne in mind that modern woman is seeking relief from housework in order to participate in the gainful activities of the family not merely out of financial necessity, but to satisfy her innate drive for increasing independence. Far more effective relief is provided by the apartment than by the individual home, particularly if the former provides centralised servicing facilities. In a poll of the Reich's league of housewives, 60 per cent declared themselves in favour of apartment house dwellings. The verdict of practising social workers indicate that on the basis of their experience they consider single homes suitable only for the highest-income bracket of the working class, while the apartment house is the only reasonable housing type for the bulk of the lower-income groups.

Experience gained in the field of housing construction with due consideration of factors other than purely economic ones has shown that the construction of individual homes cannot be expected to provide for the bulk of the working population; that, indeed, this type of housing is often actually opposed by them. It follows that well-organised, modern high-rise apartment blocks cannot be considered a necessary evil ; they are a biologically motivated type of dwelling, a genuine by-product of our age. The objections of one-sided defenders of one-family house construction on the grounds that the nature of man roots him to the soil (an assertion entirely lacking scientific proof) is in direct conflict with the intuitive preference of many persons who feel particularly at home in an elevated apartment because they prefer the greater peace in upper stories (no noise from street or playgrounds) and the unobstructed view.

BUILDING HEIGHTS. What then is the optimum height of apartment houses, three, four, five, ten or fifty stories ?

I share the view that it is sentimental self-deceit to assert that a fourth-floor apartment without elevator is in more intimate contact with 'nature' than one on the tenth floor ; it is very questionable whether the owner of an individual house with his intimate contact with the noise, odours and dust on the ground will live more quietly or healthfully than his considerably poorer colleague on the tenth floor of a soundly planned and well-equipped high-rise development. In my opinion the optimum height of an apartment house is a purely economic problem whose solution has unfortunately not yet been clarified in all respects due to lack of practical experiments.

The systematic cultivation of high-rise apartment block design and improvement of the codes, for example in regard to elevators and installations, will increase the relative construction cost with increasing number of floors, particularly due to the increasing numbers of elevators required, but the costs of streets and public utilities will decrease simultaneously. The limits of economic expediency are defined by the height beyond which the increase in construction cost is no longer compensated by savings in site and road requirements. The most economic building height will be found at this point; it depends upon the cost of land in each particular case.

LAND USE. This leads me to the question of land use, which I shall discuss on the basis of conditions in Germany. What is the prevailing situation ?

Every building code thus far has surpassed its predecessor in the attempt to improve health conditions for the inhabitants of densely populated sections, but even the newest codes bear the stamp of a fight between speculation and public authority instead of applying systematic curbs to private interests based on a farsighted, social idea rooted in the proper biological premises for wholesome dwelling conditions. Even present building codes fail to provide adequate possibilities of bringing nature to the doorstep of the residents of sections with high-density zoning. The terrible light-well apartments of the late nineteenth century were eliminated by unified postwar building codes; they were replaced by city block units of peripheral buildings surrounding an interior courtyard, the customary method of today. But this type of construction still has the great disadvantage of inadequate illumination and ventilation. The practice of surrounding the city block entirely on all sides results in unfavourable orientation with inevitable northern exposures for a large number of the apartments, as well as unsatisfactory corner solutions, with overshadowed apartments; important health requirements are thus ignored. This building code is in need of revision; particularly, however, the zoning laws. These legal changes will be dominated by emphasis on parallel instead of peripheral apartment blocks. This grouping provides considerable advantages for the site and has recently been used to an ever increasing extent. Parallel rows of apartment blocks have the great advantage over the old peripheral blocks that all apartments can have equally favourable orientation with respect to the sun, that the ventilation of blocks is not obstructed by transverse blocks, and that the stifled corner apartments are eliminated. Such parallel rows also provide for systematic separation of highways, residential streets and footwalks more easily and at less cost than in the case of peripheral construction. It makes for better illumination and more quiet, and also decreases the cost of road building and utilities without decreasing the effectiveness of land use. The over-all distribution is thus considerably functionalised, resulting in improved conditions of hygiene, economy and traffic.*

These advantages could be further increased considerably if new legislation would impose limitations on population

* Compared to the first, rather rigid, experiments in the field of a new distribution for urban dwellings, we have progressed today to a much more unorthodox and varied grouping of apartment blocks. The prevalent opinion is that the optimum of orientation has to be compromised sometimes to avoid dull regularity at all costs.

density instead of building heights, i.e., if it controlled the quantitative ratio of dwelling area or building volume to site area. Comparative studies I made reveal that *hygienic and economic conditions become more favourable in many respects as the number of stories increases, and that high-rise apartment blocks are thus superior to the conventional walk-ups of three, four or five floors with inadequate park strips between blocks and insufficient distances between window fronts.* In my comparisons I assume that both fronts of the parallel apartment blocks are to have at least two hours of sunlight on December 21, when the sun is at its lowest.

According to Heiligenthal, this leads to the rule of thumb that the distance between parallel blocks must be one and one half times the building height in the case of blocks oriented in the north-south direction, two and one half times the building height in the case of east-west orientation, and twice the building height in the case of diagonal orientation. This rule shows that north-south orientation is the most favourable in regard to efficiency of land use. Moreover, the majority of dwelling plans in Northern Europe are best suited to an east-west exposure of their two fronts. On the basis of these facts I made a comparative study of parallel blocks with north-south orientation having alternatively from two to ten stories built on a given site, and I deduced the following rules, which will serve to support my suggestions for amending the regulations concerning population density (see Fig. 40, a, b, c, d) :

1. *Assuming a site of given size and a given angle of sunlight incidence (30°), i.e., a given illumination condition, the number of beds increases with the number of stories.*

2. *Assuming a given angle of sunlight incidence and distributing a given number of beds (15 square metres or 161 square feet of area per bed) into parallel apartment blocks with varying number of stories, the size of the required site decreases with increasing number of stories.*

3. *Assuming a building site of given size and a given number of beds and varying the number of stories, the angle of sunlight incidence decreases with increasing number of floors, i.e., the conditions of illumination improve with increased height.*

For a given utilisation of the site and a given dwelling area or number of beds, the distance between apartment blocks in the case of a ten-story building has increased to almost twice the minimum distance prescribed by the rule of thumb, and that without any economic sacrifice. This is a striking gain. It is thus absurd that current legislation imposes limits on building height instead of dwelling area or building volume, which deprives the public of these obvious economic and hygienic advantages. In a ten- or twelve-storey high-rise apartment block even the ground floor occupant can see the sky. Instead of lawn strips only 20 metres (66 feet) wide, the windows face landscaped areas with trees which are 100 metres (328 feet) wide and help to purify the air as well as providing playgrounds for the children. Here nature penetrates the city and offers the urbanite new charms ; and if all roof areas were made into gardens, which has rarely been done, then the city dweller will have succeeded in reconquering the land which is lost on the ground when the house is built. *The large city must assert itself ; it requires a development of its own, a type of dwelling adapted to its own life which provides a maximum of air, sunlight and vegetation with a minimum of traffic and maintenance needs.* The high-rise apartment block is capable of fulfilling these requirements, and therefore its promotion is among the most pressing tasks of the housing policy.

ADVANTAGES AND DISADVANTAGES OF HIGH-RISE APARTMENT BLOCKS. One fear remains : the lack of a direct connection between the dwelling and the ground. The safety of elevators must be increased sufficiently so that children can use them without danger, and this is an economic rather than a technical problem. Prejudice against high-rise buildings is frequently ascribed to the difficulty of supervising children. The kindergartens of today are still no cure for this situation. Nevertheless, the well-managed, hygienically improved kindergarten (most expediently located in the landscaped areas between the parallel blocks) and the nursery for babies (located in the roof gardens) should be the proper solution. The children themselves frequently oppose group organisation, but it must be remembered that schools and hospitals once met with the same opposition. However the socialisation of the urban family is progressing irrevocably, and the democratic nature of the high-rise apartment building and of the centrally serviced household corresponds to this trend. The individual's need for seclusion, which frequently enters the argument against high-rise buildings, should not be overestimated. It is best satisfied by fulfillment of the require-ment that each adult shall have his own room, small though it may be, to which he can retire. Very much is made of mutual co-operation among families, which is of course much more readily possible in a high-rise apartment building than in an individual home. And only high-rise apartment blocks can relieve the individual occupant of a large fraction of the most tedious and time-consuming domestic chores by means of its centralised service installations ; these are also of importance from the viewpoint of national economy because of their over-all savings in material and time. Is it of no importance that the overburdened housewife in the modern industrial worker's family no longer needs to carry the coal upstairs and tend to the furnace for heat and hot water ? That the service centre handles her laundry more efficiently than she could herself ? That the advent of electric refrigerators, vacuum cleaners, mechanical ventilators, centralised kitchen installations, and finally even communal recreation rooms, sport facilities and kindergartens is approaching ? The cost of such conveniences can be distributed economically over a large number of families in a high-rise apartment block, costs whose purpose it is to transform saved time into the most valuable commodity of all : creative leisure !

I believe that the idea of high-rise apartment blocks has now been clarified and its indispensability for modern cities proven, but habits cannot be conquered by reason alone, because intel-lectual adaptation is not enough ; only practice can conquer the prevailing mentality, and we must fight in all countries in favour of the construction of high-rise apartment blocks. The first high-rise developments should be built for younger, more favourably situated families who will show a desire to test and help develop this new way of life and living. The entire hous-

FIG. 36 : The Harvard Yard. The new Graduate Centre is on top

FIG. 37 : The Harvard Graduate Centre (Architect—the Architects Collaborative, 1949).
Photo : Fred Stone, Cambridge, U.S.A.

FIG. 38 : Church in Bergamo, Italy, showing side by side Romanesque, Gothic and Renaissance building elements. *Photo : Konrad Wachsmann*

FIG. 39 : Comparison of old and new methods of block division

FIG. 40—a, b, c, d : Diagram showing the development of a rectangular site with parallel rows of apartment blocks of different heights. Conditions as to air, sun, view and distance from neighbour block are improved with increased height of the blocks in c and d. In a and b these conditions are constant, but the higher the buildings the less land is needed for the same amount of living space.

FIG. 41 : Plaza San Marco, Venice

FIG. 42

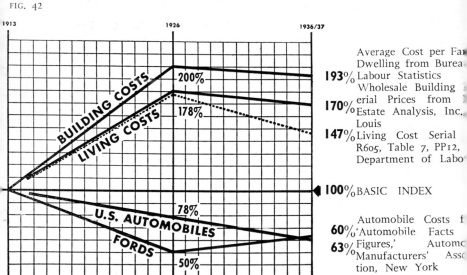

1913   1926   1936/37

BUILDING COSTS

LIVING COSTS

200%

193% Average Cost per Fa■ Dwelling from Burea■ Labour Statistics

178%

170% Wholesale Building ■ erial Prices from ■ Estate Analysis, Inc. Louis

147% Living Cost Serial R605, Table 7, PP12, Department of Labo■

100% BASIC INDEX

U.S. AUTOMOBILES

78%

60% Automobile Costs f■ 'Automobile Facts

FORDS

50%

63% Figures,' Automo■ Manufacturers' Asso■ tion, New York

FIG. 43 : A New York street—a riot of styles, forms and colours

44a : Peter Breughel, a village square. eets and squares here are still fitting eptacles for social intercourse of the ole community

FIG. 44b : But what has happened now to the pedestrian?

ing industry will then inevitably become convinced that only high-rise apartment blocks can assure the urban population of a maximum in living comfort in regard to health and transportation at a price it can afford.

To sum up :

The city dweller's choice of the type of his dwelling must be aimed at achieving the maximum value within his reach. This choice depends upon his inclinations, his occupation and his budget.

The dwelling in a house with garden offers more quiet, more seclusion, more recreation facilities and elbow room in one's own garden, and greater ease in the supervision of children; it is not economical as a minimum dwelling, its maintenance is more expensive and time-consuming, it makes for long travelling distances and ties down its occupants.

The dwelling in an apartment house ensures short travelling distances and provides economical centralised services for housekeeping and recreation ; it causes some difficulties in the supervision of children outdoors due to the vertical distances from the ground, but it is economical as a minimum dwelling and promotes community spirit.

Walk-up apartment buildings have the disadvantage of inadequate distances between them, of insufficient sunlight, narrow park strips and inadequate outdoor space. The high-rise apartment block, on the other hand, is much airier, sunnier and more separated, it provides a maximum of wide park areas in which, above all, children can satisfy their need for play and noise. It is also more favourable in regard to the cost distribution of central services.

Its advantages are decisive for healthy cities.

Hence : houses are not the panacea, and their logical consequence would be a dissolution of cities. *The aim is to deconcentrate, not to dissolve the city.* The extremes of city and country must be reconciled by making use of all our technical resources and by fully landscaping all available space on the ground and on roofs in order that nature may become a daily experience, not merely a Sunday excursion.

The construction of houses and high-rise apartment blocks must be developed simultaneously, each to the extent of its

I

real demand. Wherever possible, the house should take the form of a one- or two-storey structure in suburbs zoned for low density, while the high-rise apartment block should have an economical height of ten to twelve stories with centralised services, and it should be built wherever its effectiveness is proven, particularly in districts zoned for high density.

Walk-up apartments offer neither the advantages of the house nor those of the high-rise apartments, to which it is inferior socially, psychologically and in some respects even economically ; their elimination will be welcome progress. In the last analysis, the future relative acceptance of the two remaining types of dwelling will depend on developing social and political trends

Organic Neighbourhood Planning*

LACK OF INTEGRATED PATTERN. With the development of the machine age the coherence and efficiency of the old community, which was characterised by the crafts, has rapidly disintegrated. The absence of a well-integrated, new community pattern that would fit the changed living conditions of the machine age is the most serious drawback to the promotion of genuine democratic growth.

The body called 'society' is an indivisible entity which cannot function when some of its parts are not integrated or are being neglected; and when it does not function properly it will sicken.

GROWING SOCIAL INDIFFERENCE. The size of today's depersonalised mammoth city administrations has grown beyond human scale. A citizen of the city has no personal contact with his elected officials ; he is obliged to surrender to a distant power. Consequently, growing social indifference has slackened community relations. Irresponsibility and social loneliness are spreading. Art, science and religion today are disconnected islands ; a new synthesis must make whole again what is now, unhappily, separate.

Science, art and philosophy could supply the elements for a new order. Food, leisure and freedom could be had by all, but a workable method of collaboration and distribution has still to be found. Only when living in a well-integrated neighbourhood can the citizen of today experience and learn the democratic procedure of give-and-take. Healthy neighbour-

* See : 'A Programme for City Reconstruction' by W. Gropius & Martin Wagner, *The Architectural Forum*, New York, July 1943. *Rebuilding Our Communities* by W. Gropius, Paul Theobald, Chicago, 1945. *Organic Neighbourhood Planning* by W. Gropius, *Housing and Town and Country Planning*, Bulletin No. 2, United Nations Department of Social Affairs, Lake Success, New York, April 1949.

hood units are therefore the natural seed beds for improved human relations and higher standards of living. They help to develop a sense of community loyalty which finds expression in concerted action for social and civic progress.

Such a broad aim cannot be realised merely through 'better housing.' Housing, representing only one of many community functions, cannot be tackled unrelatedly without checking the capacity of the surrounding community to absorb new residential areas, and to provide good circulation and proper relationship between dwellings, working places and recreation areas. Otherwise our city features and techniques will begin to engulf our rural areas more and more, carrying with them the germs of our modern civic diseases : irresponsibility, deterioration of social contact, amorphous growth without coherence or distinctive form. Full consideration of an organic community plan as an indispensable framework has to precede any housing development. Without it, even new housing may turn rapidly into a blighted area and become a burdensome waste.

Sound community planning by local planning boards should be made the prerequisite of any public support for housing. Furthermore, the present trend toward decentralisation has to be carefully watched lest it should lead back to scattered and unplanned housing.

BASIC COMMUNITY PATTERN. Well-planned community rehabilitation seems to call first for drastic steps to stimulate community interest and responsibility on the part of every citizen by letting him participate actively in local affairs. To attain this goal, the administrative community framework must be humanised, that is, brought down to man size. It should be based on self-contained neighbourhood units as distinct entities small enough to serve as organisms for reactivating social intercourse. After a generation of trial and error, architects and planners everywhere have agreed on this basic community pattern for the immediate future :

The smallest self-contained community unit—basic for urban and rural areas alike—should be the 'neighbourhood unit' with five to eight thousand inhabitants, which is a population large enough to assure efficient operation of an elementary school.

The next larger administrative unit should be a precinct or district in the city or a township in the country, each comprising a cluster of from five to ten neighbourhood units—say, from 25,000 to 75,000 people—with a high school at its centre.

Finally, the largest unit should be the entire city or metropolis with top grade facilities for education and recreation.

Each self-contained neighbourhood unit should have its own independent local government.

Such a scaled-down governmental setup would secure a more direct influence of the will of the people upon their administration and would also develop a sense of community spirit. Relations between families, friends and co-operative teams would have a better chance as creative factors in ordinary living. Direct participation in the corporate life of the unit would become a natural function of every citizen and would protect him against loneliness and isolation. Disregarding some few secluded hermits, man is a gregarious animal whose growth is always accelerated and improved by life in a healthy community. The reciprocal influence of individuals on each other is as essential to mental development as food is to the body. Left alone, without neighbourly contact, the citizen's mind is dulled, its growth stunted.

THE HUMAN POINT OF VIEW. In accordance with the humanly scaled local administration, the physical scale of such an organic social structure also must be human ; that is, it must fit the cycle of the twenty-four-hour day, since men, not machines, determine the fundamental scale. Daily travelling time should total no more than thirty to forty minutes. The size of the neighbourhood unit—whether rural or urban—should be confined to pedestrian distances, for the human stride ought to define the scope of local living space. All points of activity and interest in the neighbourhood unit should be within ten to fifteen minutes' walking distance at the most. This would confine its size to an area with a radius of about one-half mile or less.

To be well balanced in itself, the basic unit requires working places for its inhabitants in separate business and industrial segments, as well as its own local administration, a shopping centre and facilities for education, recreation and worship. Not one of these should be forgotten, for housing alone—a mere conglomeration of people—does not create an organic community. However, provided with communal facilities, every part of the unit being well related in size and location, the inhabitants would have a good chance to improve social contact, the prospect of which originally made urban life desirable. The social initiative of the people and their resourcefulness in organising their own life would then originate at a local level and gradually reach out into a wider region.

NEW REGIONAL ARTICULATION. Through civic interest and loyalty growing from good relations within the immediate neighbourhood and through healthy, competitive spirit and pride in achievement, regional articulation will again develop after having been lost in the industrial upheaval of the past. Delinquency and crime will also decrease with the improved social character of the neighbourhood unit ; for it has been found that social ills result from the lack of coherence and effectiveness of the social group rather than from biological or psychological factors, or even from poverty. Thus, a neighbourhood unit, through forethought and the proper planning of well-integrated surroundings, has a good chance to build up its own identity and to retain and strengthen it. A good community plan cannot by itself create good neighbourliness, but it can provide an environment full of potentialities.

CULTIVATION OF THE SOCIAL SOIL. Such a statement has sound scientific background. Two English biologists, Dr. Scott Williamson and Dr. Innes Pearse, have done unique research in London's Peckham Health Centre. They studied the structure of society in its smallest unit, which, according to them, is not the individual but the family. They found that nowhere could biologists study health as such, for everything was directed only toward the investigation of the sick. Consequently they created a platform upon which the possibilities of a rich, diversified social life could be offered to average families, affording the biologists an undistorted view of the factors supporting normal growth. In a specially designed, club-like building with swimming pool, cafeteria, nursery, gym and playrooms, hundreds of average London families found release from their previous social isolation. No experts were admitted and all the initiative for communal activities came from social intercourse among these families. No activities were forced on them, but plenty of opportunities were provided by the right type of building. The only requirement for membership was a periodic health overhaul.

The record of their experiment shows that 'health grows and spreads not by treatment of sickness, not by prevention of disease, nor primarily by any form of correction of physical or social ills, but through cultivation of the social soil.'

According to them health, if given a chance to spread, is just as 'infectious' as disease. And they find that a community is not formed merely by an accumulation of persons for the convenience of sustaining some ulterior purpose, as in a housing project connected with a large industrial plant. Rather it is the result of a natural, functional organisation in society. As it grows, it determines its own anatomy and physiology according to biological law. Thus a community is a specific 'organ' of the body of society, formed of living and growing cells—the homes which compose it.

The heart of the communal organism, co-ordinating the potentialities for a rich, diversified life, is the neighbourhood civic centre from which branch out the social arteries that determine the character and strength of the whole group. Initially such a centre requires a meeting hall and some committee rooms and could best be developed in connection with the school. Here the people themselves can direct their daily life in contact with all age groups and have influence in the administration as well as in the cultural activities. As a social nucleus, the civic centre gives direction and stimulation to concentrated group efforts, and at the same time enables each individual, through active participation, to attain his full stature within the community.

PRIORITY FOR COMMUNITY CENTRE. *Since these small community centres are instruments of such vital importance to the human development of the group, they should be given priority over any other rehabilitation scheme, even over housing.* Like the powerhouse of an industrial plant, they generate the current for the vital arteries of the group.

Everywhere community improvement can be speeded up by adopting an organic sequence in the planning procedure, that is, by creating two essential preconditions : the setting up of new neighbourhood units, urban or rural, and their boundaries, each unit to have its independent local government; and the erection, in a central position, of a small community centre within each of these units, preferably in connection with the school building. This would establish a sound, humanly scaled framework with an immediate political significance.

PROCEDURE AND SEQUENCE IN COMMUNITY PLANNING. What sequence of procedure should we employ to break the vicious circle choking our cities? As they need relief from congestion, from 'high blood pressure,' we should first siphon out those people who cannot be permanently employed in the city and offer to resettle them, together with some smaller industries, in neighbourhood units to be built in the country. I want to emphasise that such a policy requires the transfer of endangered production as well as purchasing power from sore spots in the city to a sound new area. There stranded workers can be reclaimed for production at a much lower cost per capita than the old city would need to pay for slum clearance on expensive land and for unproductive relief. Such a transfer of idle labour would relieve the sick body of the old city, improve its circulation and open up the recreation space for its rejuvenation.

The open spaces thus regained in the city could be used for the erection of necessary communal facilities and park areas, and for a basic net of traffic arteries connecting the neighbourhood districts with each other and with the civic centres. Freed of dead weight, the reopened areas of the dying cities could then be returned to their proper functions as integral parts of an organic social structure for the whole region. Such a development would, of course, take time.

From the planning of neighbourhood units in the open country—the initial step in the process of reconstruction—we should be able to gather enough experience to manage the much more difficult second step of developing new community structures within the old cities.

SUGGESTIONS FOR A PRACTICABLE RECONSTRUCTION PROCEDURE:*

1. Lot and block rehabilitation has not been successful. Sweeping 'square mile' rehabilitation has become a necessity since we have recognised the interrelationship of the town with its region.

2. Former suggestions such as 'The City Beautiful' and other pictorial schemes have proved to be incomplete. First action should be started by preparing legal, financial and administrative instruments to enable the planners to conceive and work out reliable master plans.

3. Places of work and their relation to places of living should form the pivot of all reconstruction work.

4. First of all the existing cities should be relieved of congestion and high blood pressure by removing those who cannot be permanently employed. Resettled around small industries in new 'townships' these people would regain their productive capacity and purchasing power.

5. The new townships should settle along superhighways and be connected by fast feeder roads with the old city centre.

6. The size of the townships should be limited by the pedestrian range to keep them within a human scale.

7. The townships must be surrounded by their own farm belts.

8. Speculation often promotes blight and obsolescence. Therefore the community should own the land. The dwelling lots should be rented, though the house may be owned.

9. The administrative setup of a township should take the

* From : 'A Programme for City Reconstruction' by Walter Gropius & Martin Wagner, *The Architectural Forum*, July 1943.

form of a self-contained unit with its independent local government. This will strengthen community spirit.

10.   From five to ten—or more—neighbourhood townships may be combined into a countyship with an administration governing activities beyond the reach of a single unit. Its size and administrative setup should also serve as a model for the basic neighbourhood units of the old towns to be reconstructed.

11.   It is suggested that the size of a township remain stable. Flexibility within its boundaries must therefore be achieved by making the housing facilities elastic.

12.   Parallel to the resettlement of idle labour in new townships, a second process must take place ; acquisition of land by the community of the old city. For not until that process of pooling land has been completed can the next step—the redistribution of land—be taken for the final reconstruction of the city.

A fundamental framework as outlined above would constitute a sound basis for building up a town pattern fit for the twentieth-century machine age from the social as well as from the economic and cultural points of view.

Problems of the 'Core'
(Community Centre)*

I am deeply convinced that *the building of community centres is of even greater urgency than housing itself, for these centres represent a cultural breeding ground which enables the individual to attain his full stature within the community.*

Different countries have found different answers to what actually constitutes a community centre, a 'core,' according to their varying hereditary habits and traditions, their stage of technical development and the natural setting in which they find themselves. The Latin countries, for instance, have, early in their history, developed clearly defined plazas in which the life of the community centred and found its expression, while the Anglo-Saxon civilisation has made comparatively little use of such public centres, favouring, instead, the individual home as meeting ground for most social intercourse.

This is, of course, partly due to the difference in climatic conditions, but not entirely so. Regional preferences and imponderables must be given careful consideration when attempting new solutions and, in many cases, it will be necessary first to reawaken a demand for community centres because they have disappeared from the scene to such a degree that people do not even remember their great advantages for the individual and the communal life.

In former, more settled periods of history such public centres grew either naturally by public demand or by decree of a potentate, but they were never neglected as they are so often in the present, particularly in those countries that stand in the forefront of industrial and technical development. While we equip the individual home with every conceivable amenity

* See : CIAM, *The Heart of the City*, Pellegrini & Cudahy, New York, 1952.

we have overlooked the merits of the public meeting place ; we have surrendered our streets and public spaces almost entirely to the automobile, and the pedestrian, forced to withdraw to a narrow pavement, has lost his right of way. The important neighbourly contact which had been so basic for the coherence of the old cities and towns has been destroyed by the explosive force of vehicular traffic. It is important that we should re-establish in our communities public centres where people, undisturbed by traffic, can rub elbows in a neutral atmosphere that is not dominated by the influence of the private home and where the spirit of the community can find its public expression.

The most famous example of a beautiful core which for centuries has served its community most effectively as receptacle for its public life is the Piazza St. Marco in Venice. It expressed the greatness of God in its cathedral, the power of the doge in its palace; the tower was a symbol the sailors could see from the sea; but most of all it was the big drawing room of the people, the public stage of the town for festivities, parades and religious ceremonies. When we look at the modern plaza in front of the United Nations buildings in New York we find that it is hardly used as a community centre; it is more a monumental approach to the entrances. Rockefeller Centre in New York offers a small community core which promotes some exchange between people, but its value is impaired by the roar of traffic passing by. In a modern city plazas for pedestrians seem to be more necessary than ever before, for here, in daily contact and exchange among people grow the grass roots of democracy.

Why does one core within a town or city attract us as pleasant when another may not ? The intricate problem of scale lies at the bottom of this question. A good solution much depends on whether a harmonious relationship has been achieved between the height of the surrounding buildings and the dimensions of the plaza. The actual size of the plaza should barely accommodate the peak hour of activity. If it is too large it will look empty and may never provide the contagious atmosphere and liveliness so essential for its success. Gigantic.

undivided open spaces leave most people intimidated rather than stimulated.

I have found that if a harmony has been created between open spaces and surrounding building masses such a well-balanced composition can even absorb discordant details. In the cores of old towns we find also that very different individual buildings, often centuries apart and of different styles, are living side by side in complete harmony as parts of an organic whole. This harmony, however, is not the result of a 'matching,' process; the design of a new building which was to be added to the existing old ones was invariably conceived as part of the greater whole into which it had to fit harmoniously, but contemporary means of expression were used, not borrowed style motives of past periods.

One problem that inevitably arises in connection with the planning of community centres is whether its buildings should have a 'monumental' expression. The controversy over the definition of monumentality and whether monuments are an 'eternal' need of mankind is obviously caused by the acute drama of transformation of all our inherited values that our generation is faced with. Disregarding the pseudo-monumentalism of imitative eclecticism which is slowly coming to a halt like a flywheel whose motoric force has long since died, the accepted meaning of the word 'monument' is a memorial of huge size, symbolising something worth commemorating—religious faith, an important event, a great man, a social accomplishment. *Rather than on its size I should like to put the emphasis on the spiritual meaning of a monument, on its artistic conception and grandeur, on those intangibles which are likely to stir the imagination.* The very idea of resuming monumental expression through static form symbols as in the past should be alien to the creative mind of our period. The monument of former times was the symbol for a static conception of the world, replaced today by a new one of relative values. I believe, therefore, that the equivalent for monumental expression will develop in the direction of a new physical pattern for a higher form of civic life, a pattern characterised by its adaptability for continuous growth and change. To give a more concrete example for such a statement : The Tennessee Valley Development in the United States, representing a new, collective effort to organically improve the whole setup of a community and its administration, will, I believe, contribute more toward a monumental expression of our time and will inspire more civic self-respect and loyalty than the imposing size of an Empire State Building, a mere quantitative symbol of expediency.

But higher spiritual aspirations of a growing culture, reaching beyond utilitarian aspects and worth to be visibly interpreted by the architect and the artist, develop only slowly, subconsciously. When the prevailing philosophy of 'time is money' will yield to a humanly higher civilisation—then the reconquest of the 'monumental' will be at hand. But it will not come back as the 'frozen music' of static symbols; it will become, instead, an inherent quality of our whole man-made environment.

Housing Industry[*]

Man is undoubtedly endowed with the capability of building his dwelling soundly and adequately, but innate inertia and sentimental attachment to tradition are obstructing his progress. The austerity occasioned by world events is today forcing governments as well as individuals to surmount this inertia. By adjusting to changed world conditions, attempts are finally being made to realise the old ideal of building typical dwellings more cheaply, better and in larger numbers than heretofore so as to provide every family with the basis for a healthy life. Generally applicable solutions genuinely suited to modern conditions have not yet been found, simply because the problem of dwelling design as such has never been dealt with in its entirety of sociological, economic, technical and formal ramifications. Starting from scratch, it must be solved on a large-scale basis by a systematic consideration of these factors. All previous attempts were deadlocked on controversial side issues, on matters of 'ersatz' materials and economy construction measures, on agricultural or aesthetic deliberations. However, as soon as the over-all scope of preconcieved requirements which affect the dwelling design problem are clearly recognised and accurately outlined, the tactical problem of realisation is reduced to a mere problem of methods and large-scale management.

This universal ideal of 'how do we want to live?' as a generally applicable result of reflections upon the spiritual and material possibilities of our age has not yet been clearly outlined. The chaotic lack of unity of our residential buildings is

---

[*] See: Bauhausbücher, Vol. 3, *Ein Versuchshaus des Bauhauses*, Albert Langen Verlag, Munich, 1924.

Though this article was written thirty years ago I have included it in this book, because I still consider it essentially valid after extended practical experiences in prefabrication.

evidence of the vagueness of prevailing concepts concerning the proper dwelling for modern man.

Is it a reflection of man's way of life that each individual's dwelling should differ entirely from that of every other individual ? Is it not a sign of intellectual impoverishment and fallacious thinking to furnish a dwelling in rococo or Renaissance style while identical modern clothes are worn in all parts of the world ? Advances in technology made during the past three generations surpass those of millennia before us. The better we organise physical labour, the more the human spirit will be emancipated. Perhaps mobile dwellings which will enable us to take with us all the conveniences of comfortable living even when we move are no longer utopian.

Housing the people is a problem of mass requirements. Who would dream of having his shoes custom made ? Instead, we buy stock products which satisfy most individual requirements, thanks to refined production methods. Similarly, it will be possible for the individual in the future to order from stock dwellings suitable for his purposes. Modern technique might already be ripe for this development, but the building trade today is still using old methods of handcrafts in which the machine plays only a subordinate role. A radical reformation of the entire building trade along industrial lines is therefore a must for a modern solution of this important problem. It must be simultaneously approached from the three angles of economy, technology and form; all three are interdependent. Satisfactory results can only be gained by simultaneous progress in all three fields because of the profusion of complex problems involved. These are beyond the competence of the individual and can be solved only by a concerted effort in collaboration with numerous experts.

Reduction of cost of dwelling construction is of decisive importance for the national budget. Attempts to reduce the cost of conventional handicraft methods of construction by introducing more rigorous organisational techniques have brought only slight progress. The problem was not attacked at its root. The new aim, on the other hand, would be the manufacture by mass production methods of stock dwellings which are no longer constructed at the site but are produced in special factories in the form of component parts or units suitable for assembly. The advantages of this method of production would be increasingly greater in the extent to which it becomes possible to assemble such prefabricated component parts of houses at the building site just like machines. This dry assembly method, to be discussed in detail below, would eliminate not only the troublesome twisting and warping of building parts due to moisture but also the loss of time required for the drying out of houses built by conventional construction methods of masonry, mortar and plaster. This would at once ensure independence of weather and season.

An industrial building process of this type is only conceivable on a broad financial basis. The small individual contractor engineer or architect will never be in the position to realise such building techniques alone by himself. On the other hand, large enterprises involving all the separate branches under a single ownership have been found to be economically feasible in other fields of business as well. It would therefore be necessary first to mobilise a large number of interested people before consumer organisations and vertical enterprises could be formed whose financial strength would be adequate to ensure the realisation of such a major project. Of course, the economic advantages of this industrialised construction method would then be enormous. Experienced experts estimate that savings of 50 per cent or more can be expected. This would imply that every employed person could then afford to provide his family with a good, healthful dwelling, just as he can nowadays purchase the articles of daily need at less cost due to the development of world industry than this was possible for previous generations. The cost of these industrial products could be reduced step by step by the use of steam and electric power increasingly replacing hand labour ; cost reduction in the construction industry will equally depend upon the exploitation of such power.

The other important means of cost reduction is based on new farsighted financing policies which should consciously avoid excessive interest rates on the building capital due to unproductive middlemen dispensable in the transaction.

Before decisive preliminary organisational steps can be

K

taken toward solving the industrial mass production problem, our living requirements must be clarified sufficiently to establish generally valid, precise demands as to 'how do we want to live?' As a result, numerous habits will be found to be superfluous and obsolete ; for example, it should be no loss to reduce the size of rooms in favour of increasing living comforts. *The majority of citizens of a specific country have similar dwelling and living requirements ; it is therefore hard to understand why the dwellings we build should not show a similar unification as, say, our clothes, shoes or automobiles.* The danger of undesirable suppression of legitimate individual requirements should be no greater here than in the case of fashions.

There is no justification for the fact that every house in a suburban development should have a different floor plan, a different exterior of a different style and different building materials ; on the contary, this is a wasteful and tasteless attitude of parvenus. The old farmhouse as well as the average citizen's town house of the eighteenth century, for example, all throughout Europe, show a similar arrangement of the floor plan and the over-all design. However, the danger of too rigid a standardisation, such as is exemplified by the English suburban home, must be avoided because suppression of individuality is always shortsighted and unwise. Dwellings must be designed in such a way that justified individual requirements derived from the family size or the type of profession of the family head can be suitably and flexibly fulfilled. *The organisation must therefore aim first of all at standardising and mass-producing not entire houses, but only their component parts which can then be assembled into various types of houses, in the same way as in modern machine design certain internationally standardised parts are interchangeably used for different machines.* The production policy would provide for carrying in stock all individual parts necessary for the construction of houses of various types and sizes, to be ordered to the building site as required from various specialised factories. At the same time field-tested assembly plans for houses of different layout and appearance will be available to the public. Since all the standardised machine-made parts will fit together accurately, house erection at the site on the basis of precise assembly plans can be performed rapidly and with a minimum of labour, partly with unskilled workers, and under any conditions of weather and season. Above all, this method avoids once and for all the numerous embarrassing surprises and unpredictable hazards which are inevitably connected with the conventional methods of construction : failure of building elements to fit due to inaccurate wall dimensions or to the effects of moisture, unforeseen patchwork due to construction damage, loss of time and rent due to delays in drying, as well as the consequences of the usual haste in the design of custom-made house plans. Instead, we shall be blessed with exact fit of the various machine-made component building parts, with a fixed price, and with a brief, accurately predictable and guaranteed assembly time for the house.

The realisation of this economic and organisational scheme is above all the engineer's problem. Also from his point of view the task represents a radical change from conventional developments in regard to building materials as well as structural design. Most construction today is executed with the old natural building materials, stone, brick and wood. Production of most of the old house takes place at the building site. The necessary tools and machinery, while being transported to the site for this purpose, block the traffic. These mobile factories, so to speak, are necessarily primitive compared to stationary plants. Erection of the building shell by conventional methods makes it impossible to predict the time required for the rough enclosure to dry and the interior to be completed because this depends upon weather conditions. Attempts to perfect these conventional building methods, for example by enlarging the building blocks and introducing more highly standardised and efficient organisation of the work at the site, failed to achieve significant simplifications or cost reductions. In order to reap the advantages of the new assembly construction methods, industry will therefore have to employ building materials other than those used heretofore, materials capable of being processed by machine instead of unprocessed natural materials. In this respect the aim would not be the creation of substitutes, but the improvement of natural products to obtain absolutely reliable uniformity of performance (rolled steel, cement alloys, synthetic wood). A standardised solution of the problem would be made possible only by prefabrication of all the structural parts necessary in the construction of a house, even the walls, ceilings and roof.

To this end, the structural design of houses must also be changed drastically. Either a material must be produced which possesses the same structural and insulating properties as conventional masonry walls while having less volume and weight so that it can be assembled in large slabs of story height, or else the whole structure must be made of a structural skeleton on the one hand and of non-structural wall, roof and ceiling panels on the other. A skeleton of this type may be of steel beams and columns or of reinforced concrete beams and pillars connected to different structural systems similar to wood frame constructions. The panels for the walls, ceilings and roof will have to consist of standardised slabs which are to be factory-made of weather-resistant material, dimensionally stable, yet porous, insulating, tough and of light weight. Building slabs of this nature are already beginning to appear on the market in the form of the conventional planks of pumice concrete or gypsum. But the problems involved in the industrial production of satisfactory wall, ceiling and roof panels, as well as of a suitable light skeleton for houses, are still in need of an economical solution. The standardisation and mass production of doors, windows, stairs, trim, fixtures and interior finish has already reached a more advanced stage of development, although hand labour still outweighs industrial machine production. The engineer engaged in vehicular design for railroad cars, ships, automobiles and aeroplanes has surpassed the building engineer in the development of his methods of construction and materials insofar as he has already perfected the use of machine-processed, homogeneous building materials (iron, aluminium, glass) and the application of machine-produced structural components made of such materials. His experience is therefore of inestimable value in the field of housing mass production.

The new building method should meet with approval from

the artistic standpoint as well. *It is fallacious to assume that architecture will deteriorate because of the industrialisation of dwelling construction. On the contrary, the standardisation of building elements will have the beneficial effect of imparting a unified character to new dwellings and developments.* There is no reason to fear monotony such as that of English suburbs, provided the basic requirement is fulfilled of standardising only the building elements, whereas the appearance of buildings assembled from these elements will vary. The form of these elements shall be determined solely by their purpose and function. Their 'beauty' should be ensured by good, well-finished materials and lucid, simple design, not by added-on decorations and profiles alien to their structural or material properties. The success with which these building elements, this large-scale 'erector set,' are assembled into an actual structure of well-proportioned space depends upon the creative talents of the designing architect. The standardisation of parts certainly does not limit the variety of individual arrangements which we all desire, and the recurrence of individual parts and identical materials in the various buildings will have a rhythmic and soothing effect on us. Adequate freedom remains for individual or national character to express itself, exactly as in the case of our clothing, and yet all of it will bear the stamp of our era.

As extensive a project as the industrialisation of building construction can only be carried out with the aid of an unusual extent of public support. The problem is of such great importance to national economy that laymen and experts alike must emphatically demand that the government make preparations for its solution on a public level. States and communities, being the major builders, are compelled economically and culturally to exploit all possible means for reducing the cost of housing construction. The previous approach of encouraging the use of 'ersatz' materials and short-cut methods of construction has failed to reach the goal. Publicly supported experimental building sites are needed ! Any article to be mass-produced by industry must be systematically subjected to numerous preliminary tests in which the businessman, the engineer and the artist participate equally before its model is standardised for production ; similarly the production of standardised building components can be accomplished only by large-scale collaboration among industrialists, economists and artists. Teamwork so organised, not the creation of 'ersatz' methods, would represent genuine planning and economic foresight.

It is obvious that construction of the pilot model houses will require considerable investment, just as do the models made in industrial laboratories as a basis for mass-produced consumer goods. The financing of these experiments is the task of the consumer organisations which are to benefit from the savings to be achieved ultimately. They are the organisations primarily interested in the establishment of experimental institutions where all previous accomplishments can be systematically collected in accordance with guiding principles and be tested with a view to the new building rationale. So drastic a modification of the building industry is bound to take place gradually, to be sure. But in spite of all arguments against such development, it will inevitably come. The enormous waste of materials, time and labour, caused by the fact that extensive housing developments are still being built by hand according to countless unrelated individual designs instead of being mass-produced according to standardised though flexible plans, can no longer be defended on any grounds.

A Way Out of the Housing Confusion*

The idea of eliminating waste by rationalisation has permeated the modern life of communities and individuals alike. But rationalisation must not be mixed up with ability to produce profit, for social requirements of the population, as well as economic problems, are involved.

The rationalisation of building should imply collecting, concentrating and unifying all isolated efforts for the various building activities in order to obtain a general plan covering the building field.

Creative research for improvement and refinement can become effective only by systematic organisation of the existing material and mental equipment applied to the process of building and by their mutual inter-relation. Most delay in the progress of modern building is caused by lack of unification.

Housing, the most urgent and also the most complicated building problem, illustrates this statement strikingly : Today, the main task of the building profession—socially and technically—is to build up an adequate service to provide sufficient, decent, up-to-date dwellings for the community. These buildings, which have to satisfy the material and psychical requirements of life, must be constructed at the lowest possible expense of time and material, and at a price the average man can afford. Is this sort of dwelling on the market ? No, it is not. Although the average man buys his food, his clothing and his other everyday goods at a reasonable price, adapted to his income, the only dwelling he can obtain is an obsolete building originally built for more wealthy people, and now out of date. Even the rent of government-supported housing develop-

---

* See : 'Toward a Living Architecture' by W. Gropius, *American Architect & Architecture*, New York, February, 1938. *Memorandum for the House Committee Investigating National Defence Migration* by W. Gropius & Martin Wagner, U.S. 77th Congress, 1st session, 1941, Vol. 17, pp. 6949-56.

ments with public subsidy is still too high to be afforded by the lower-income class.

Something must be wrong with the whole building trade if the rent of even these dwellings, only about half paid for by their tenants, remains out of reach of the poorest. Here it becomes evident why the market is not interested in building dwellings for the average man in spite of the wide demand. Prices and rents, which give the builders and owners of dwellings a good profit, are far out of proportion to the prices of all the other articles in daily use which are well adapted to the average income. What is the reason for this devitalising process ? What must be changed in the economic structure in order to rebalance the market price of adequate dwellings ?

In 1928, I found in the U.S.A. a most illuminating diagram, roughly comparing the trend of prices for building and for automobiles between 1913 and 1926. It shows the remarkable fact that within the same period the average costs of building were doubled, whereas the price of the Ford car was halved. The greater proportion of handwork involved in building increased the price in accordance with the increasing labour costs. Refinement of mass production methods, on the other hand, considerably lowered the price of automobiles. A decent dwelling became unattainable for the low-income class, yet the car became an everyman's tool. The up-to-date completion of the diagram shows that the price of the average car has steadily declined, whereas the cost of the average dwelling has been only slightly lowered since 1926. This diagram reveals that our building methods, being far behind the times, are not yet fit to solve the problem.

As building is the most extensive and complicated field of human production, it could not keep pace with the development of the machine—and it is the last field to be conquered by it. Further, there is no balanced organisation of the building trades yet, as there is in other industries ; it is still rather tied up with handwork and individual management which, forced into competition with industrial methods, have lost their former quality and efficiency. Although more and more parts of the building are constantly being made by machine, progress is hampered by lack of comprehensiveness, with which this problem should be attacked as a whole. For this is not a problem of mere manufacturing. Surely mass production methods must eventually permeate the building trade ; but deep changes in the economic structure are indispensable before the market will be ready for prefabrication on a large scale. The first enthusiasm toward prefabrication has calmed down, after many drawbacks have given evidence that no single person or single firm alone can solve that gigantic task as Ford solved it for the automobile. The solution of this problem seems to be self-evident ; yet, it is so deeply rooted in our economic structure that the community as a whole can master it only by attacking it from all angles simultaneously. It is, first of all, a problem of integration. Much time will be gained, therefore, if a comprehensive scheme of action is set up by the best experts, co-operating in all the many fields of building activity. A guiding key plan offers authoritative significance which should direct the future efforts toward housing. The many brilliant private efforts, now lost by isolation and lack of power, must be united.

It is obvious that private enterprise, in its struggle for existence, is bound to over-emphasise subjective interests. A public institute, however, would be apt to investigate more objectively all sorts of ideas and inventions and their practicability for the good of the commonwealth. Only technological approach, undisturbed by any political or private interference, can set a high standard.

An 'Institute of Building Integration' should be created, in which federal, state and municipal authorities would co-operate with architects, engineers, contractors, manufacturers, realtors, bankers and trade-unionists as their advisers, to produce a final solution of the pressing need for adequate housing. All the existing institutions for public and private research in building practice should co-operate, exchanging their experiences and results, simultaneously acquiring a better knowledge of the difficulties of correlated problems. The key plan to be set up by such an institute would aim at embracing everything expected to raise the social standard, to decrease the prices of houses, and to secure their movability in accordance with the fluctuation of the working places. Primary considerations would involve :

Regulating regional planning by inter-state legislation, e.g., zoning ordinances.

Furthering the lease of land for housing for limited periods.

Preparing the investment market for prefabrication and for the new idea of a housing service (shorter amortisation and lower interests).

Improving building regulations by adapting them to new building techniques.

Research for socially and economically most suitable types of dwelling.

Research for suitable standard sizes of the component parts of dwellings ; these parts to be interchangeable for different types of houses.

Research for actual prefabrication, including mechanical units such as kitchen, bathroom, heating and air-conditioning plant.

Simplification of the building organisation in offices and at the site.

There are many brilliant attempts made in these various fields, but they are rather isolated from one another instead of being parts of a well-tuned organism which is so badly needed. The suggested Institute of Building Integration should fill this gap but, as so much organisation work would be involved, the idea of rationalisation must be safeguarded against red tape which would stunt its only aim—namely, to promote creative progress.

The cost of such an institute to be put up by the government, would be irrelevant when compared with the savings to be expected from economising on housing costs throughout the country by such means of concentration and integration. The efficiency of money spent for housing could probably be doubled and bring the key problem of social welfare close to its final solution, simultaneously increasing private initiative and employment.

IV

Scope of Total Architecture

Scope of Total Architecture*

CENTURY OF SCIENCE. I have tried to summarise for myself what the changes are that have taken place during my own lifetime in the physical as well as in the spiritual world. When I was a boy, my family lived in a city apartment with open gas jets, individual coal-heated stoves in each room, including the bathroom, where warm water was heated for the bath each Saturday : that took two hours. There was no electric tram, no automobile, no plane. Radio, film, gramophone, X-ray, telephone were non-existent.

The mental climate which prevailed in the eighties and nineties was still more or less of a static character. It rotated around a seemingly unshakable conception of eternal truths. How rapidly has this conception been fading away, changing into that of a world of incessant transmutation, of mutually dependent phenomena. Time and space have become coefficients of one and the same cosmic force.

The sum of all these tremendous changes that took place during the last half-century of industrial development has achieved a more sweeping transformation of human life than those of all the centuries since Jesus Christ combined. Small wonder, then, that we feel the strain of this superhuman speed of development which seems to be out of step with the natural inertia of the human heart and with our limited power of adaptation.

Every thinking contemporary searches his mind now trying to figure out what may be the ultimate value of our stupendous scientific progress. We roar with new techniques and new inventions for speedier means of transportation. But what

* See : *Architecture and Design in the Age of Science* by W. Gropius, The Spiral Press, New York, 1952. *Rebuilding Our Communities* by W. Gropius, Paul Theobald, Chicago, 1945. *Faith in Planning* by W. Gropius, *Planning, 1952*, American Society of Planning Officials, Chicago.

do we do with all the time saved ? Do we use it for contemplation of our existence ? No, we plunge instead into an even more hectic current of activity, surrendering to that fallacious slogan : time is money. We obviously need a clarification as to what exactly our spiritual and intellectual aims are.

Some time ago I read an article by Leo Tolstoy in which he reproaches science for studying purposely 'everything.' He held that mankind cannot possibly pay attention to 'everything' and that we are going to tear ourselves to pieces, trying to go in a hundred different directions at the same time, unless we find out what we want most and make that the goal of our supreme effort. Of course, he thought of religion giving that final direction which establishes beyond a shadow of a doubt what should come first, after which everything else falls into place almost automatically. Well, if it isn't religion, what is it ? Science has come a long way since Tolstoy's time and there are people who seriously believe that it can be the final arbiter and pass judgment on good and evil. Even if we should come to believe this, we would still have to make up our mind as to which scientific concept we want to give free rein, because, applied simultaneously, they may easily force each other out of existence and we would be the losers.

STRATEGIC AIM. I should like, therefore, to attempt to outline the potential strategic aim of planning for my own profession, architecture, within the cultural and political context of our industrial civilisation. I shall try first to give a definition : *Good planning I conceive to be both a science and an art. As a science, it analyses human relationships ; as an art, it co-ordinates human activities into a cultural synthesis.* I want to put the emphasis particularly on the art of planning. Here, I believe, lie waiting creative potentialities that would give meaning and direction to our countless, isolated efforts.

We talk so much about the fact that the rapid development of science has cut so sharply into the familiar pattern of our existence that we are left with nothing but loose ends. In his eternal curiosity man learned to dissect his world with the scalpel of the scientist, and in the process has lost his balance and his sense of unity. Our scientific age, by going to extremes of specialisation, has obviously prevented us from seeing our complicated life as an entity. The average professional man, driven to distraction by the multiplicity of problems spread out before him, seeks relief from the pressure of general responsibilities by picking out one single, rigidly circumscribed responsibility in a specialised field and refuses to be answerable for anything that may happen outside this field. A general dissolution of context has set in and naturally resulted in shrinking and fragmentating life. As Albert Einstein once put it : 'Perfection of means and confusion of aims seems to be characteristic of our age.'

TASK OF REUNIFICATION. But there are indications that we are slowly moving away from over-specialisation and its perilous atomising effect on the social coherence of the community. If we skim the mental horizon of our present civilisation, we observe that many ideas and discoveries are wholly concerned with finding again the relationship between the phenomena of the universe, which scientists had so far viewed only in isolation from neighbouring fields. Medicine is building up the psychosomatic approach to treatment of diseases, acknowledging the mutual interdependence of psyche and soma, the body. The physicist has contributed new knowledge of the identity of matter and energy. The artist has learned to express visibly with inert materials a new dimension—time and motion. Are we on the way to regain a comprehensive vision of the oneness of the world which we had taken apart ? In the gigantic task of its reunification, the planner and architect will have to play a big role. He must be well trained not ever to lose a total vision, in spite of the infinite wealth of specialised knowledge which he has to absorb and integrate. He must comprehend land, nature, man and his art, as one great entity. In our mechanised society we should passionately emphasise that we are still a world of men, that man in his natural environment must be the focus of all planning. We have indulged our latest pets, the machines, to such an extent that we have lost a genuine scale of values. Therefore, we need to investigate what makes up the really worth-while relationships among men, and between men and nature, instead of giving way to the pressure of special interests or of shortsighted enthusiasts who want to make mechanisation an end in itself.

Whom are we going to house ? The people, of course, and that includes everybody. It injures the functions of our whole society if we neglect any part of it. The sickness of our present communities is the pitiful result of our failure to put basic human needs above economical and industrial requirements.

THE 'COMPOSITE' MIND.   If we envisage the strategic goal of planning in its vast complexity, it indeed embraces the civilised life of man in all its major aspects : the destiny of the land, the forests, the water, the cities and the countryside ; the knowledge of man through biology, sociology and psychology ; law, government and economics, art, architecture and engineering. As all are interdependent, we cannot consider them separately in compartments. *Their connectedness directed toward a cultural entity is undoubtedly of greater importance for success in planning and housing than finding ever so perfect practical solutions for limited objectives.* If we agree on this rank order, then the emphasis must be on the 'composite mind,' as we may call it, developed through a process of continuous cross-checking and balancing, rather than on the specialised expert who shuns responsibility for the whole and divides his brain in tight compartments. During all the tedious, painstaking steps that make up his daily work, his crucial responsibility is undeviatingly to keep the broad strategic aim in mind, namely, to make segmental planning part of the total.

INDIVIDUAL   FREEDOM   AND   COLLECTIVE ACTION.   For people of totalitarian states the idea to pursue simultaneously individual freedom and collective action may appear quite incompatible. They don't believe that it is feasible to combine a variety of form and thought with mass production of goods and with an orderly frame of law. Democracy, recognising the autonomy of the human spirit, makes the respect for individual variety foremost in any attempt to establish a common goal, a common denominator.

laws or regulations. Intervention of government in the affairs of the people should not mean the destruction of individualism, but rather the means of preserving it. In contrast to this attitude we witness today what is happening when organisation and planning under dictatorial regimes are becoming ends in themselves. Man is ploughed under and individual genius is paralysed in the labyrinth of subordinated offices, forced to comply with the will of the self-appointed dictatorial authority. This spectacle can only strengthen our belief that democratic government in its true form must be the servant of the people. Planning, then, should grow from the ground up, not from the top down by force ; ideas are put into action by individual initiative, not by bureaucratic edict.　Democracy represents a widening-out, centrifugal force. A feudal or authoritarian system is, on the contrary, a centripetal force, a straitjacket which stunts natural growth. The danger, emanating from the antidemocratic forces, has doubtlessly increased in our shrinking world with its widening net of communications and propaganda that has made all men neighbours in spite of any imaginary curtains.

LACK OF MORAL INITIATIVE. But we should not look for danger only in subversive quarters. I believe that we must assume a much more positive attitude in trying to keep creative impulses active and effective against the deadening effect of mechanisation and over-organisation right within the democratic societies. Our high-pressure, push-button civilisation is exerting a terror all of its own. It seems to fall short of the high democratic goal of living in pursuit of happiness. We obviously have not found the bond yet that would hold us together for a concerted effort at establishing a cultural denominator which would be strong enough to grow into a commonly recognised form of expression, both physically and spiritually. The great avalanche of science and progress has left the individual bewildered and restless, unable to adjust himself and often pitifully lacking in moral initiative. We have developed a Gallup Poll mentality, a mechanistic conception ; we rely on quantity instead of on quality, on memory instead of on ideas ; we yield to expediency instead of forming a new conviction.

ARTIST: PROTOTYPE OF 'WHOLE MAN.' Is there an antidote to this trend ? Our society has certainly recognised the essential value of the scientist for its survival. We are very little aware, however, of the vital importance of the creative artist when it comes to controlling and shaping our environment. In contrast to the process of mechanisation, the work of the true artist consists of an unprejudiced search for expression that symbolises the common phenomena of life. This requires that he take an independent, uninhibited view of the whole life process. His work is most essential for the development of a true democracy, for he is the prototype of 'whole' man ; his freedom and independence are relatively intact. His intuitive qualities should be the antidote against over-mechanisation, apt to rebalance our life and to humanise the impact of the machine. Unfortunately the artist has become the forgotten man, almost ridiculed and thought of as a superfluous luxury member of society. *My belief is that, on the contrary, our disoriented society badly needs participation in the arts as an essential counterpart of science in order to stop its atomistic effect on us.*

Examining our own experiences, we know that it is only in isolated cases that sober scientific facts can, all by themselves, stir the imagination to a point where people become willing to subordinate cherished personal ambitions to a common cause. Much deeper chords must be struck than those reached by analytical information if we want to call forth an enthusiastic, contagious response, capable of sweeping away barriers that stand now in the way of better planning and housing. Though scientific progress has reached us in the form of materialistic abundance and physical well-being, it has rarely matured into producing form. Consequently we find that our emotional demands remain unsatisfied by the mere material production of the eight-hour working day. This failure to gladden the soul must be the reason why we have not always been able to make our brilliant scientific and technical achievements count, and why a cultural pattern that should have emerged has, so far, eluded us.

I am convinced, therefore, that the contribution of the creative designer whose art can realise more fully the visual aspects and the human appeal of planning is essential. No society of the past has produced cultural expression without the participation of the artist ; social problems cannot be solved through intellectual processes or political action only. I speak of the great necessity to recover through every man's education the lost quality of understanding and creating form.

Think of those essential imponderables, apparent in cities and towns of bygone cultures, which still have the power to move us emotionally today, though they are obsolete from the point of view of practical use. These imponderables characterise what is missing in the concept of our present communities, namely, that unity of order and spirit which is forever significant, visibly expressed in space and volume.

LACK OF RESPONSIVE AUDIENCE. Can a child, growing up in 'Main Street,' be expected to be in the habit of looking for beauty ? He hasn't met with it yet and wouldn't even know what to ask for because his perceptive faculties have been blunted from the beginning by the ruthless assault of the chaotic colours, shapes and noises of modern salesmanship. He is left in a constant state of sensorial apathy, finally hardening into that intractable citizen who has ceased to be even aware of his impoverished surroundings. As often as not it is from this background, though, that the potential architectural client emerges, and it becomes immediately evident why he so rarely rises above creating anything but a blur or a sham when trying to give form to his environment.

None of our magnificent, practical new tools can turn 'Main Street' into a beautiful pattern for living unless they are put into creative hands, unless a changing attitude of mind will bring about a fusion between science and art. But at which end shall we start to bring this about ? Because what we need is not only the creative artist, but a responsive audience and how are we going to get it ? Only by a slow educational process, providing comprehensive experience from early childhood on. It means, in short, that we must start at the kindergarten to make children playfully reshape their immediate environment. For participation is the key word in planning. Participation sharpens individual responsibility, the prime factor in making a community coherent, in developing group vision and pride in the self-created environment. *Such educational conception would put book knowledge in its right place, as an auxiliary only to experience in action, which alone can lead to constructive attitudes and habits of thought.* Any information given to a citizen after he has been exposed as a youth to educational practices that made planning seem everybody's concern will fall on fertile ground.

Planners experience in their daily work that the public is still very ignorant of the great benefits awaiting it from good planning. The average citizen is inclined to see an interference with his personal freedom when given direction by government agencies. The necessity continuously to inform him why communal planning is to his own best advantage calls for the highest psychological ability in a planner. A systematic psychological training in 'basic politics' should give the planning student the understanding of cause and effect of human behaviour. It should teach him how to put into his own practice persuasion, tact, patience and appreciation of the thought and position of others as the most effective tools of planning. It should tend to give him greater flexibility of mind, the resiliency of an alert wrestler, always ready to adjust to unpredictable situations. It should fulfil the need to develop a definite attitude of the student beyond his acquisition of the necessary knowledge and techniques.

Today we still meet too often with a deep-rooted inclination to dodge a large-scale conception for planning and housing and to add up, instead, unrelated piecemeal improvements. This will change only with a growing community spirit, carefully nurtured on all educational levels until it becomes a subconscious attitude of everybody and may finally cause a chain reaction conducive to solving our collective task.

NEEDED: EXPERIMENTS IN LIVING. Such an educational framework, as here indicated, also seems to have qualities favourable for the advancement of genuine team-work which will naturally develop more and more in the future with the ever widening horizon of our physical know-ledge of which each of us commands only a small segment. The task is too big for individuals alone. After almost twenty-five years of most valuable research and formulation of our ideas, we seem now to be in urgent need of action in groups. For in spite of the wealth of theoretical thought on community living which has been accumulated in recent years, hardly any new comprehensive 'experiments in living' have been made. There is no other way toward progress but to start courageously and without prejudice new practical tests by building model communities in one stroke and then system-atically examining their living value. What a wealth of new information for the sociologist, the economist, the scientist and the artist would be forthcoming, if groups, formed of the most able planners and architects available, should be com-missioned to design and build completely new model com-munities ! Such information would also offer most valuable preparatory data to solve the complicated problem of rehabilit-ating our existing communities. The blocks which have to be removed before we can create such laboratories for living are obviously political and legal in character. Without duly accepted legal instruments, one community master plan after the other will become a symbol of wishful thinking, of agonising frustration.

I would propose also to bring to its test in these model units the much debated problem of how to keep more power of administrative decision down at the local level of the small self-contained unit. For any device to create more favourable conditions for direct participation of the citizen in the running of his community is essential for the attainment of an organic solution.

NOMADIC TREND. I remember that during a conven-tion of the International Congress for Modern Architecture (CIAM) the question was raised by European architects whether Americans would ever be capable of creating a pattern for sound community life on a modern basis comparable to the closely knit townships that dominated the European picture before the advent of the machine. It was argued that the nomadic trend of the American population was so disruptive that nothing but makeshift arrangements could be expected and all local flavour would be destroyed by this mass of vacillating people in pursuit of the dollar. An American planner who was present * answered this challenge by telling of an experience he had had when he moved with his family to a place in Vermont that had always attracted him. He thought he had picked a town with the most pungent Vermont flavour, only to find, after some investigation, that the majority of the people were, like himself, born and raised elsewhere, but had selected Vermont as the place where they most wanted to live. They had come out of preference and had absorbed the local colour to an astonishing degree. He felt that young Americans were not prepared to sit it out in the same towns where their parents and grandparents lived, as the Europeans have done for so many centuries ; that, on the contrary, they usually became quite resentful when forced to do so. But, if given the chance to get around and look at as many regions as possible, they finally picked out one to settle down in permanently which for various reasons appealed most to them and then often became more co-operative and enterprising citizens than those who had never stirred from home. Now, if we can conceive of the future citizen as a person willing to contribute wherever he happens to settle down instead of merely looking for the easiest opening and the quickest gain, then we have, maybe, found an answer to this baffling spectacle of a nation whose citizens are, voluntarily or involuntarily, so much on the move.

To help this development we must conceive contemporary community features which would exert so stimulating an influence on the citizen who comes to live there that he will soon change from an onlooker into a participator. Such a desirable trend could well be brought about by a campaign to recapture the right-of-way for the pedestrian. As we all know, every citizen is both, now a driver, now a pedestrian ; but

---

* Martin Meyerson, Assistant Professor of City Planning, University of Pennsylvania.

while everything is being done for the car and its driver, the pedestrian has been pushed against the wall in the process of building up the great net of automotive traffic which has exploded our communities. I am convinced that it is just as necessary, or even more so, now to create, in addition, independent pedestrian traffic nets, separate and protected from the automobile. Such a superimposed pedestrian path pattern should start and end, not at a strung-out main-street, but in a beautiful plaza, prohibited for cars, the very heart or core of the unit, to serve as the local centre for the exchange of public opinion and participation in community affairs. Here, from daily social intercourse in trade and recreation, from gossip on local and world news, grow the grass roots of politics. Such a pedestrian square of human scale with its centralised social purpose would give the inhabitant a feeling of belonging and pride. It would prepare him for the sharing of responsibility, for conscientious voting and for his taking an interest in community planning which the planner needs so badly for future action. This is an ardent plea for the modern community core, the most vital organ to promote democratic process.

HUMAN SCALE FOR THE CITY. I so strongly emphasise the small self-contained unit with its community centre because new experience here, on the smallest scale, will throw new light also on the more complicated problem of the larger cities and the metropolis. It will help in the gigantic task of humanising them. For the problem of the big cities is certainly not one of building only new civic centres or piecemeal housing. It is evident that nothing less than a complete overhaul of their sclerotic bodies can turn them into healthy organisms again. We all know that their congested areas are hungry for open spaces, for nature, light and air, that their citizens long for a recognition of their identity, while the city itself needs to be protected at the same time against individual encroachment. I do not intend to elaborate on the social, political and economic procedures and implementations to reach this goal. But I wish to stress the great need of more systematic research also on the metropolitan level. How can we recapture in the city, socially and physically, the completely destroyed human scale ? Research has to precede the necessary action. The growth of a living urban organism can be channelled into a superior civic form by the planner and architect only if its social functions have been recognised by new legislation, built up on the results of that preceding research. Existing law is mostly obsolete and insufficient for twentieth-century urban life, and most countries have as yet failed to put the emphasis on the whole of the communal organism, on its context rather than on its separate parts.

'HOUSING' IS NOT ENOUGH. If we try to appraise the physical achievements in housing and in organic community set-up during the last twenty years, we can safely state that in several countries plan and construction of the individual family dwelling or apartment has been greatly improved with respect to livability and level of standard, but there is hardly any so-called 'development' which would appeal to us as a true community, balanced in itself. Developments usually show just a quantity of streets and houses, accumulated in an additive manner without such communal features as would transform a mere housing scheme into a purposely limited, well-sized organism. They may be made up of pleasant, individual houses and often present an admirable economical achievement, but the layout of the town is usually but a dull, unimaginative conglomeration of endless strings of houses. It utterly lacks the stimulation that might have been attained from those intangibles of creative beautiful design and total conception which give life its deeper value and for which the past has given us magnificent examples of unity.

As to the conception of the contemporary dwelling itself we must first start by checking up on our own attitude toward the human and psychological components of the problem and its ever changing aspects. Only a mature mind with deep understanding of the physical and psychological requirements of family life is able to conceive a shell for living to be efficient, inexpensive, beautiful and so flexible that it will be adequate for the ever changing life cycle of the family in all its stages of growth.

OUR HABITAT. However, the greatest responsibility of the planner and architect, I believe, is the protection and development of our habitat. Man has evolved a mutual relationship with nature on earth, but his power to change its surface has grown so tremendously that this may become a curse instead of a blessing. How can we afford to have one beautiful tract of open country after the other bulldozed out of existence, flattened and emptied for the sake of smooth building operations and then filled up by a developer with hundreds of insipid little house units, that will never grow into a community, and scores of telephone poles added in place of the thoughtlessly cut trees ? Native vegetation and the natural irregularities of the topography are destroyed by negligence, greed or lack of ideas, because the average type of developer regards the land first of all as a commercial commodity from which he feels entitled to reap a maximum profit. *Until we love and respect the land almost religiously, its fatal deterioration will go on.*

The human landscape which surrounds us is a broad composition in space, organised from voids and volumes. The volumes may be buildings or bridges or trees or hills. Every visible feature in existence, natural or man-made, counts in the visual effect of that great composition. Even the most utilitarian building problems, like the location of a highway or the type of a bridge, are important for the integrated balance of that visible entity which surrounds us. Who else but the creative planner and architect should be the legitimate, responsible guardian for our most precious possession, our natural habitat, for the beauty and adequateness of our living space as a source of emotional satisfaction for a new way of life ? What all of us seem to need most in this hectic rush we have let life slide into is an ubiquitous source of regeneration which can be only nature herself. Under trees the urban dweller might restore his troubled soul and find the blessing of a creative pause.

I have come to the conclusion that an architect or planner

worth the name must have a very broad and comprehensive vision indeed to achieve a true synthesis of a future community. This we might call 'total architecture.' To do such a total job he needs the ardent passion of a lover and the humble willingness to collaborate with others, for great as he may be he cannot do it alone. The kinship of regional architectural expression which we so much desire will greatly depend, I believe, on the creative development of teamwork. Abandoning the morbid hunt for 'styles' we have already started to develop together certain attitudes and principles which reflect the new way of life of twentieth-century man. *We have begun to understand that designing our physical environment does not mean to apply a fixed set of aesthetics, but embodies rather a continuous inner growth, a conviction which recreates truth continually in the service of mankind.*

GEORGE ALLEN & UNWIN LTD
London: 40 Museum Street, W.C.1

Auckland: 24 Wyndham Street
Sydney, N.S.W.: Bradbury House, 55 York Street
Cape Town: 58–60 Long Street
Bombay: 15 Graham Road, Ballard Estate, Bombay 1
Calcutta: 17 Chittaranjan Avenue, Calcutta 13
New Delhi: 13–14 Ajmere Gate Extension, New Delhi 1
Karachi: Haroon Chambers, South Napier Road, Karachi 2
Toronto: 91 Wellington Street West
São Paulo: Avenida 9 de Julho 1138–Ap. 51

A SHORT DICTIONARY OF ARCHITECTURE

Dora Ware and Betty Beatty

This is a practical reference book, not only for students of architecture, but for everybody whose work or interests bring them into contact with the building industry, and its array of technical terms. Nearly every term in current use in architecture and building has an historical origin, and Miss Ware's definitions and Miss Beatty's drawings constitute a miniature historical survey of European architecture. It will be equally useful to the student who is wholly concerned with modern methods of building and architectural design, to the amateur who finds architecture interesting as a subject, and to professional men like structural and civil engineers and surveyors.

Third Edition Revised & Enlarged

Demy 8vo   12s. 6d. net

A SHORT DICTIONARY OF FURNITURE

John Gloag

The Scotsman described it as 'a very useful work of reference for collectors and students of domestic history,' and said also : 'the value of the dictionary is enhanced by the extensive use of drawings. . . . It is preceded by two essays on the nomenclature and design of furniture, and followed by lists of British and American makers. The concluding section provides in tabular form an outline of materials, styles, and fashions from 1100 to 1950.'

In *The Architect's Journal*, 'Astragal' said : 'This is a fascinating book. . . . There are 640 illustrations, all of them excellent. They include, as they should, a number from *Punch.*'

The Times Educational Supplement said it was 'a handy and remarkably comprehensive reference book on a small scale. He has managed to include a reference to almost every aspect of furniture in England since 1100, and also in North America since the middle of the seventeenth century.'

The *Furniture Record* : 'A "must" for both the amateur or the professional dealer in furniture.'

Demy 8vo   42s. net

INDUSTRIAL ART EXPLAINED

John Gloag

First published in 1934, Mr. Gloag's compact survey of industrial art has for years been accepted as one of the chief standard works on the subject. The original edition was confined to British industrial design ; but the new enlarged edition includes many examples of contemporary work in the United States. The book has been re-written, and several new sections added, including one on the relationship of materials to industrial design.

New and Enlarged edition, with 48 plates in colour and black and white, and many illustrations in the text, from original sources and specially drawn.

Demy 8vo 15s. net

SELF-TRAINING FOR INDUSTRIAL DESIGNERS

John Gloag

This book takes the student of design on from the point where he has completed his training in an art school or a technical college. It suggests courses of study which will familiarise him with industry and industrial processes ; tells him how he can set about applying the technical training he has received, and extending it, and using it in the most practical way in his day-to-day contact with commerce and business. Above all, the thirteen chapters of this book are planned to help the young designer to get well started on the road to being a professional designer.

Cr. 8vo 8s. 6d. net

ADVERTISING EXPLAINED

Denis Caton

It explains, in simple language, the various elements which go to the making of a successful advertising campaign—the planning, research and discussion—and gives some helpful information about advertising media, the creation of advertisements, about printing processes and mechanical production.

Cr. 8vo 8s. 6d. net

THE PLACE OF GLASS IN BUILDING

Edited by John Gloag

Christian Barman, Kenneth Cheesman, Richard Sheppard,
Lionel B. Budden, G. A. Jellicoe, E. M. S. Wood,
Grey Wornam

This book has been planned primarily for students of architecture and building and constitutes a practical illustrated guide to the chief types of glass manufactured in Great Britain, and includes descriptions of their properties and appropriate uses. Architects, Engineers and Surveyors will also find this book a useful and handy work of reference.

Third Enlarged and Revised Edition

10s. 6d. net

BUILDING FOR DAYLIGHT

Richard Sheppard, Hilton Wright, John Gloag

A comprehensive and detailed examination of design in relation to the admission of daylight to buildings, covering domestic, civic, commercial and industrial architecture. Detailed specifications for the use of glass in various types of buildings are given, including housing, schools, hospitals, stores, canteens, railway stations, hotels and swimming baths. With many illustrations in half-tone, line and colour.

Demy 4to   21s. net

CONFERENCE ON TROPICAL ARCHITECTURE

*A Report of the Conference held at
University College, March 1953*

Among the papers reprinted here, together with subsequent discussion, fully illustrated with plans and photographs, are: *Tropical Planning Problems, Indian Climate and Thermal Comfort in the Tropics, Tropical Architecture and Buildings Standards, The Natural Lighting of Buildings by Refected Sunlight, Style and Tropical Architecture, Traditional Materials*, etc., etc. Authors include Sir William Holford, O. H. Koenigsbager, P. Johnson-Marshall, Arthur Foye, Frank Ruther, Ore Arup, and T. C. Angus.

11″ x 8½″   32s. net

INDUSTRY IN TOWNS

Gordon Logie

Gordon Logie, A.R.I.B.A., author of *Furniture from Machines*, here turns his attention to one of the most pressing problems in Town Planning to-day—that of the proper place of industry in our towns. He writes from the standpoint of a town planner who realizes that factories are just as important as houses and schools, and that if industry does not prosper, all our schemes for urban reconstruction must fail through lack of the necessary resources.

In the course of his researches he has visited hundreds of factories to get the necessary facts at first hand. Almost as a by-product he describes in simple terms the manufacture of such varied objects (to paraphrase Lewis Carroll) as "ships and needles and silverware ; chocolates and glue."

The illustrations include photographs of most of the best recent industrial buildings in this country and abroad. They show how great an architectural transformation is possible, and that, given the necessary goodwill, an industrial area can become one of the showplaces of a town.

Cr. 4to   60s. net

PLANNED PACKAGING

Harry Jones

Opening with a brief discussion of the relations between packaging and industrial design the author then gives a concise history of the development of packaging in Great Britain, showing how the early conception of a package as something needed only to protect the contents was changed, by the appearance of branded goods, into recognition of the package as a potent force in every sales campaign.

In the second half of his book he considers the effect of the war on British design and lists some of the remarkable American war-time developments—Stripcoat, Pliofilm, Metalam, etc. He condemns the complete lack of training facilities in Great Britain and makes suggestions for the provision of training schools. Lastly he examines all the factors needed to design a good package—material, appearance, colour, copy, etc. The 96 illustrations of package designs are particularly valuable in a book which will be of the greatest interest to all designers, manufacturers, advertising agents and students.

Cr. 4to   35s. net

WORLD PERSPECTIVES

'The aim of *World Perspectives* is to present short books written by the most conscious and responsible minds of today. Each volume sets forth the interrelation of the changing religious, scientific, artistic, political economic and social influences upon man's total experience . . . The authors deal with the increasing realization that the body and the spirit are not separate and apart ; that intuition and reason must regain their importance as a means of perceiving and fusing inner being with outer reality.' RUTH NANDA ANSHEN Series Editor.

APPROACHES TO GOD
Jacques Maritain

Jacques Maritain is one of the greatest living Catholic philosophers. In *Approaches to God*, he examines critically the methods by which man comes to know his Creator. There are as many paths to God, he says, as there are by-ways on earth, or roads to the human heart. Those who know him from other books, such as *The Degrees of Knowledge* and *Creative Intuition in Art and Poetry*, will recognize in this one the qualities of thinking and exposition which have given him pre-eminence in the field of Christian philosophy.

Cr. 8vo   8s. 6d. net

WORLD INDIVISIBLE
Konrad Adenauer

The appearance of this book by Europe's brilliant elder statesman is fresh evidence of the scope and authority of *World Perspectives*. Dr. Adenauer has recorded in these pages the essence of his political philosophy, of his experience in government over many years, particularly as the head of a powerful nation during the most critical period of its history.

Cr. 8vo   10s. 6d. net

RECOVERY OF FAITH
Radhakrishnan

In this inspiring book, one of the most brilliant of modern philosophers and statesmen gives an aswer to man's need for a new faith.

Cr. 8vo   Cloth 12s. 6d. net; paper 8s. 6d. net

GEORGE ALLEN & UNWIN LTD